1st EDITION

Perspectives on Modern World History

Student Movements of the 1960s

1st EDITION

Perspectives on Modern World History

Student Movements of the 1960s

Alexander Cruden

Editor

GREENHAVEN PRESS
A part of Gale, Cengage Learning

New Lenox
Public Library District
120 Veterans Parkway
New Lenox, Illinois 60451

GALE
CENGAGE Learning·

Detroit • New York • San Francisco • New Haven, Conn • Waterville, Maine • London

Elizabeth Des Chenes, *Director, Publishing Solutions*

© 2012 Greenhaven Press, a part of Gale, Cengage Learning.

For more information, contact:
Greenhaven Press
27500 Drake Rd.
Farmington Hills, MI 48331-3535
Or you can visit our Internet site at gale.cengage.com.

For product information and technology assistance, contact us at
Gale Customer Support, 1-800-877-4253.

For permission to use material from this text or product, submit all requests online at
www.cengage.com/permissions.

Further permissions questions can be e-mailed to permissionrequest@cengage.com.

Articles in Greenhaven Press anthologies are often edited for length to meet page requirements. In addition, original titles of these works are changed to clearly present the main thesis and to explicitly indicate the author's opinion. Every effort is made to ensure that Greenhaven Press accurately reflects the original intent of the authors. Every effort has been made to trace the owners of copyrighted material.

Cover image © Jeff Albertson/Terra/Corbis and © Janine Wiedel/Photolibrary/Alamy.

LIBRARY OF CONGRESS CATALOGING-IN-PUBLICATION DATA
Student Movements of the 1960s / Alexander Cruden, book editor.
   p. cm. -- (Perspectives on modern world history)
   Summary: "Student Movements of the 1960s: The series provides basic historical information on a significant event in modern world history, presents the controversies surrounding the event, and provides first-person narratives"-- Provided by publisher.
   Includes bibliographical references and index.
   ISBN 978-0-7377-6372-0 (hardback)
   1. Student movements--History. 2. College students--Political activity. I. Cruden, Alex.
   LA186.S77 2012
   378.1'981--dc23   2012013295

Printed in the United States of America
1 2 3 4 5 6 7 16 15 14 13 12

CONTENTS

Saying that the Communists of Asia threaten the United States, the president doubles the size of the draft that requires young men to join the military. He declares Vietnam is where the battle for US freedom must be fought.

CHAPTER 2   Controversies Surrounding Student Movements of the 1960s

vatives, student radicals were more interested in sex than politics, and antiwar activists were pro-violence. Even the rock music of the supposedly liberal time celebrated anti-Christian and anti-women values.

FOREWORD

*"History cannot give us a program for the future,
but it can give us a fuller understanding of ourselves, and of our common humanity, so that we
can better face the future."*
                                    —Robert Penn Warren,
                                    American poet and novelist

The history of each nation is punctuated by mo-
mentous events that represent turning points for
that nation, with an impact felt far beyond its bor-
ders. These events—displaying the full range of human
capabilities, from violence, greed, and ignorance to heroism, courage, and strength—are nearly always complicated and multifaceted. Any student of history faces the
challenge of grasping the many strands that constitute
such world-changing events as wars, social movements,
and environmental disasters. But understanding these
significant historic events can be enhanced by exposure
to a variety of perspectives, whether of people involved
intimately or of ones observing from a distance of miles
or years. Understanding can also be increased by learning about the controversies surrounding such events
and exploring hot-button issues from multiple angles.
Finally, true understanding of important historic events
involves knowledge of the events' human impact—of
the ways such events affected people in their everyday
lives—all over the world.

Perspectives on Modern World History examines
global historic events from the twentieth-century onward
by presenting analysis and observation from numerous
vantage points. Each volume offers high school, early
college level, and general interest readers a thematically

arranged anthology of previously published materials that address a major historical event, with an emphasis on international coverage. Each volume opens with background information on the event, then presents the controversies surrounding that event, and concludes with first-person narratives from people who lived through the event or were affected by it. By providing primary sources from the time of the event, as well as relevant commentary surrounding the event, this series can be used to inform debate, help develop critical thinking skills, increase global awareness, and enhance an understanding of international perspectives on history.

Material in each volume is selected from a diverse range of sources, including journals, magazines, newspapers, nonfiction books, personal narratives, speeches, congressional testimony, government documents, pamphlets, organization newsletters, and position papers. Articles taken from these sources are carefully edited and introduced to provide context and background. Each volume of Perspectives on Modern World History includes an array of views on events of global significance. Much of the material comes from international sources and from US sources that provide extensive international coverage.

Each volume in the Perspectives on Modern World History series also includes:

- A full-color **world map**, offering context and geographic perspective.
- An annotated **table of contents** that provides a brief summary of each essay in the volume.
- An **introduction** specific to the volume topic.
- For each viewpoint, a brief **introduction** that has notes about the author and source of the viewpoint, and that provides a summary of its main points.
- Full-color **charts**, **graphs**, **maps**, and other visual representations.

- Informational **sidebars** that explore the lives of key individuals, give background on historical events, or explain scientific or technical concepts.
- A **glossary** that defines key terms, as needed.
- A **chronology** of important dates preceding, during, and immediately following the event.
- A **bibliography** of additional books, periodicals, and websites for further research.
- A comprehensive **subject index** that offers access to people, places, and events cited in the text.

Perspectives on Modern World History is designed for a broad spectrum of readers who want to learn more about not only history but also current events, political science, government, international relations, and sociology—students doing research for class assignments or debates, teachers and faculty seeking to supplement course materials, and others wanting to improve their understanding of history. Each volume of Perspectives on Modern World History is designed to illuminate a complicated event, to spark debate, and to show the human perspective behind the world's most significant happenings of recent decades.

INTRODUCTION

In 1960, young people did not have much say. Countries were run by older men. Dwight Eisenhower, seventy, was president of the United States. Its main rival, the Soviet Union, was led by Nikita Khrushchev, sixty-six. The British prime minister, Harold Macmillan, was also sixty-six. The leader of France, Charles de Gaulle, was seventy. Japan, China, and Germany were led by men ages sixty-four, sixty-seven, and eighty-four, respectively.

The world of business followed the same pattern. So did the academic world. In the United States and elsewhere, the older generations took charge across all major areas of society, and it was almost always male-dominated. The prevailing spirit of the times is captured perfectly in the title of one of the most popular TV shows of the 1950s, *Father Knows Best*.

In the 1960s, that all changed explosively—and the detonators were college students. Sparked by the injustice and hypocrisy they saw on campuses and in the world at large, students not only supported but led what became powerful movements that challenged the old order. Throughout the decade students crusaded for human rights, peace, freedom, and education reform while exposing the flaws of their elders.

Not all students were part of these movements. Many were at times sympathizers, activists rarely, and for the most part frequently concerned with other matters, like studying. Many students opposed the liberalism of the activists; many more tried to avoid the whole set of controversies, simply desiring degrees and then jobs. And more than a few used protest movements as excuses for wild self-indulgence.

Yet one thing that made the decade so extraordinary was the maturity shown by a range of student leaders. It was not just the energy of youth that burst forth in the 1960s, it was a combination of intelligence and morality applied fiercely to major issues in society and government.

On reflection, the outbreak of such intelligence should not have been a surprise. Among the US college students of the 1960s, expectations ran high. Their parents had survived the Great Depression, won the greatest war the world had ever seen, and participated in an economy that seemed to ensure growth forever. These students were brought up in an aura that assumed success, were brought up amid the ideals of freedom, justice, and prosperity, and were told their potential was unlimited.

Then, on the campuses, especially at large universities, they slammed into limits. The bureaucracy of big universities seemed indifferent to their unique potentials. Corporate conformity overruled individualism. In particular, for students of color and for women, the daily reminders of unequal treatment painfully contradicted the ideals of their textbooks. Many students felt they had no choice but to accept the situation. Yet a remarkably large number decided they could not. As activist student Jo Freeman put it in her book *At Berkeley in the Sixties*: "We found much to do and fully expected to do it all."

Students on the front lines of the struggle for civil rights risked their scholarships, degrees, careers, and even their lives, yet generally kept their cool and made their case with thoughtful logic and nonviolent bravery. Certain young women took the same route in order to expose the widespread social and workplace inequalities of being female. Students across the country applied their intellectual skills in shaping demands for more relevant instruction in the colleges they were paying to attend.

The activism of students grew along with US involvement in the Vietnam War. As the 1960s continued, US presidents committed more and more troops to defending South Vietnam, a small and far-off nation where the US government claimed American support was necessary to stop communism from taking over all of Southeast Asia. This meant more and more young American men were being drafted into the armed forces and sent into a war that the United States, despite its superior technology, was finding increasingly difficult to win.

Opposition to the draft ranged from personal desperation to principled appeals. Protests against the war took many forms, sometimes lawless. Yet, just as in the campaigns for civil rights, large numbers of students who were not directly affected by the war became active against it. This substantial commitment well beyond self-interest separates the student movements of the 1960s from student activism in previous eras.

Earlier student movements were chiefly small, localized protests involving issues close at hand—and not of high principle. Perhaps the earliest American campus rebellion came at Harvard in 1766, when students staged a walkout over rancid butter in the dining hall. J. Angus Johnston writes in *Student Protest: The Sixties and After* that in the early 1800s, students at such prestigious institutions as Princeton and the University of Virginia from time to time violently opposed administrators' attempts at discipline, but after the Civil War, colleges became peaceful and "student self-government caught hold." Administrators were "channeling students' hunger for power and relevance into the service of the status quo."

The pattern of student self-interest and administration co-option continued on into the twentieth century. In the 1930s, up to half a million students participated in strikes against war, but then divisions over the influences of communism and fascism—on the rise in Europe and Asia—splintered student opinion. World War II rendered protest moot; as Johnston writes, "campus-based activism virtually disappeared after Pearl Harbor." In 1960, though, it burst open in strikingly diverse and eventually powerful ways.

Through their idealistic maturity and their commitment to causes beyond narrow self-interest, students of the 1960s helped bring about changes that still reverberate half a century later, in the United States and around the world. As Leonard Gordon puts it in the *Encyclopedia of Sociology*, "the far-reaching Civil Rights Act of 1964, the public shift from support of to opposition to the Vietnam War, and the pressure to diversify college student bodies and curricula racially and ethnically all involved student protest-induced changes that have affected the lives of people throughout American society."

The protests and resulting changes are explored in the viewpoints of *Perspectives on Modern World History: Student Movements of the 1960s*. What comes across is the extraordinary individualism of young activists committed to a new version of American democracy.

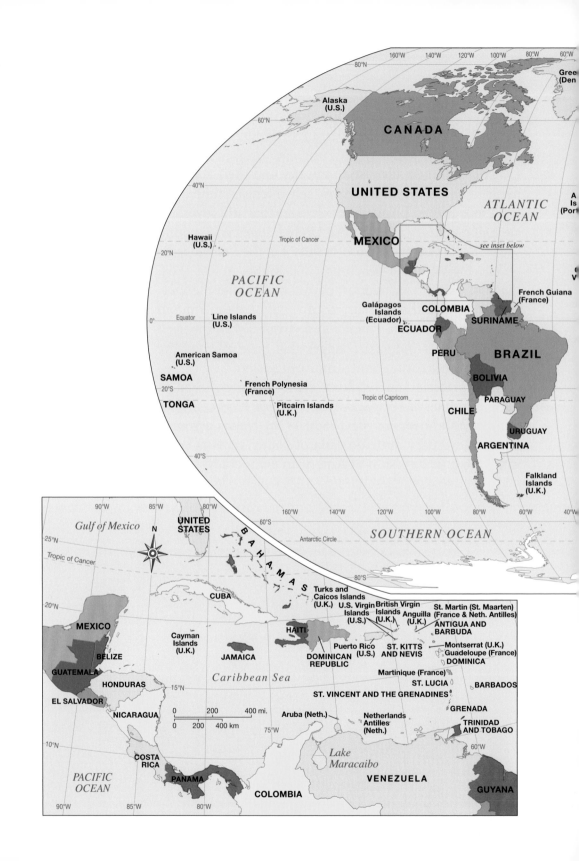

80°N

160°W   140°W   120°W   100°W   80°W   60°W

Gree
(Den

Alaska
(U.S.)

60°N

CANADA

40°N

UNITED STATES

ATLANTIC
OCEAN

A
Is
(Por

Hawaii
(U.S.)

MEXICO

see inset below

Tropic of Cancer

20°N

French Guiana
(France)

PACIFIC
OCEAN

Galápagos
Islands
(Ecuador)

COLOMBIA

SURINAME

V

0°   Equator   Line Islands
(U.S.)

ECUADOR

American Samoa
(U.S.)

PERU

BRAZIL

SAMOA

BOLIVIA

20°S

French Polynesia
(France)

Tropic of Capricorn

PARAGUAY

TONGA

Pitcairn Islands
(U.K.)

CHILE

URUGUAY

ARGENTINA

40°S

Falkland
Islands
(U.K.)

160°W   140°W   120°W   100°W   80°W   60°W   40°W

60°S

SOUTHERN OCEAN

Antarctic Circle

80°S

90°W   85°W   80°W

UNITED
STATES

Gulf of Mexico   N

25°N

Tropic of Cancer

B
A
H
A
M
A
S

Turks and
Caicos Islands
(U.K.)

CUBA

St. Martin (St. Maarten)
(France & Neth. Antilles)

U.S. Virgin British Virgin
Islands   Islands   Anguilla
(U.S.)   (U.K.)   (U.K.)

ANTIGUA AND
BARBUDA

20°N

MEXICO

Cayman
Islands
(U.K.)

HAITI

Puerto Rico
(U.S.)

ST. KITTS
AND NEVIS

Montserrat (U.K.)
Guadeloupe (France)
DOMINICA

BELIZE

JAMAICA

DOMINICAN
REPUBLIC

GUATEMALA

Caribbean Sea

Martinique (France)

HONDURAS   15°N

ST. LUCIA

BARBADOS

EL SALVADOR

ST. VINCENT AND THE GRENADINES

0   200   400 mi.

GRENADA

NICARAGUA

0   200   400 km

75°W

Aruba (Neth.)

Netherlands
Antilles
(Neth.)

TRINIDAD
AND TOBAGO

60°W

10°N

COSTA
RICA

Lake
Maracaibo

PACIFIC
OCEAN

PANAMA

VENEZUELA

GUYANA

COLOMBIA

90°W   85°W   80°W

CHAPTER 1

Historical Background on the Student Movements of the 1960s

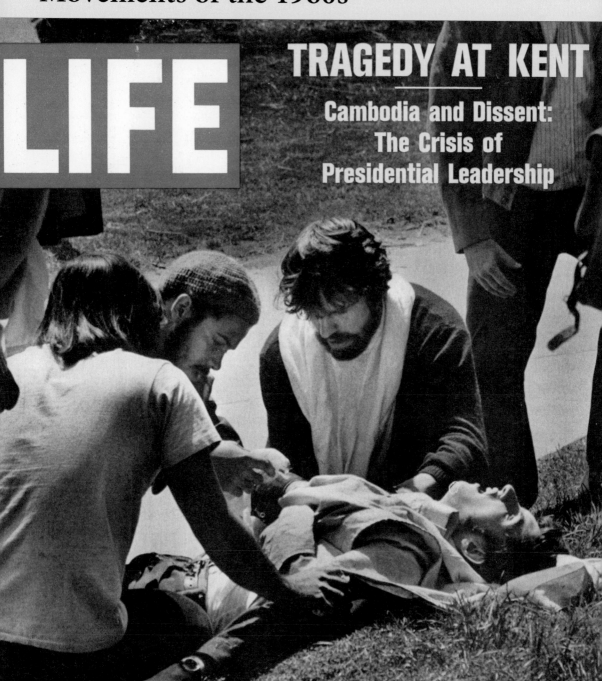

LIFE

TRAGEDY AT KENT

Cambodia and Dissent:
The Crisis of
Presidential Leadership

An Overview of US Student Activism in the 1960s

American Decades

The 1964 demonstrations at the University of California Berkeley campus set the tone and solidified major issues of the student protest movement that would sweep the United States during the decade, according to the following overview. The Berkeley administration, like that of other major universities across the country, represented conservative, government-oriented attitudes, the overview explains. As demonstrations against this authority grew, so did the number of students arrested by police called in by the university. Protesters formed the Free Speech Movement, and opposition to the military draft erupted.

Photo on previous page: Fellow students gather around John Cleary, one of nine people wounded and four killed by National Guardsmen at Kent State University in May 1970, in this photo appearing on the cover of *Life* magazine. (**Time & Life** Pictures/Getty Images.)

SOURCE. "Campus Protests," *American Decades*, vol. 7: 1960–1969, edited by Judith S. Baughman et al. Detroit: Gale, 2001. Reproduced by permission.

During the 1960s the baby boomers—the largest generation of young Americans in the history of the nation—reached college age; and, as a result of the general affluence of the United States in the years following World War II, more potential students were in a position to take advantage of higher education than ever before. Between 1955 and 1970 the number of college students nearly tripled, from 2.4 million to 6.4 million; nearly half a million instructors and researchers were employed by the nation's universities by the end of the decade, up from less than 200,000 twenty years before. In large part the explosive growth of the nation's academic community was made possible by the financial support of the federal government, specifically the Department of Defense, for whom American schools were often the laboratories where the cold war battle for technological superiority over the Soviet Union was waged. In 1961 nearly half of all federal research funds came from the Department of Defense and the Atomic Energy Commission. According to Kenneth Heineman, by the end of the 1960s schools such as the Massachusetts Institute of Technology and the University of Michigan had hundreds of defense-related contracts worth millions of dollars annually; in 1969, "the Pentagon underwrote 80 percent of MIT's budget."

The role that the academic community played in that partnership between government and defense contractors known as the military-industrial complex tended to contribute to a conservative atmosphere on campuses. Many of the administrators of the country's state universities were corporate executives or federal bureaucrats rather than educators. By the early years of the 1960s, about the time that university enrollments began to swell with the arrival of the first baby boomers, there were indications that students and faculty were questioning the values that the administrations of their schools seemed to represent.

The First Big Uprising Came in Berkeley

The first incidence of a major student revolt against a school's administration took place in 1964 on the Berkeley campus of the University of California system, which was a major supplier of military research. At the beginning of the 1964–1965 academic year Berkeley student organizations were informed that they could no longer give political speeches or pass out literature on social issues on the grounds of the student union. Although students who had raised funds on the campus for the civil rights movement saw the new rule as primarily aimed at them, all student political groups, liberal and conservative, stood to suffer from it. A broad coalition was formed among the groups affected, and on 17 September the United Front petitioned the administration to allow continued use of the student union as long as certain rules were followed. While they waited for a response, the United Front set up tables at the union as usual and began an all-night protest vigil on 21 September. The administration stood its ground, and a series of demonstrations followed, drawing support from students who had never been politically active before.

On 30 September, when eight students were issued citations from the school for continuing to man tables at the union, several hundred of their peers signed a petition saying that they were equally responsible. Demanding that they be punished as well, they occupied Sproul Hall, sitting in the building's corridors for the rest of the day and all night. While there the demonstrators planned their next moves and argued with administrators. One demonstrator, a junior in philosophy named Mario Savio, proved to be an especially compelling speaker. When a school official claimed that the new rule was to preserve political

> One demonstrator, a junior in philosophy named Mario Savio, proved to be an especially compelling speaker.

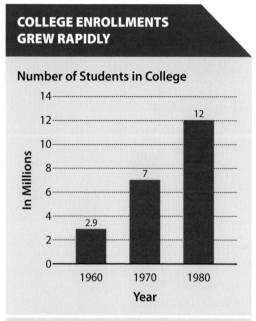

COLLEGE ENROLLMENTS GREW RAPIDLY

Number of Students in College

In Millions

14
12 — 12
10
8 — 7
6
4
2.9 — 2.9
2
0

1960   1970   1980

Year

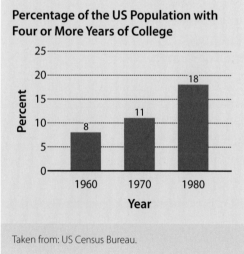

Percentage of the US Population with Four or More Years of College

Percent

25
20
18 — 18
15
11 — 11
10
8 — 8
5
0

1960   1970   1980

Year

Taken from: US Census Bureau.

neutrality on campus, Savio responded, "The University of California is directly involved in making new and better atom bombs. Whether this is good or bad, don't you think . . . in the spirit of political neutrality, either they should not be involved or there should be some democratic control over the way they're being involved?" For the demonstrators the issue was not one of political neutrality but of free speech.

The next day, 1 October, another demonstration was held on the steps of Sproul Hall, and Jack Weinberg, who was not enrolled as a student but was manning the table of the campus chapter of the Congress of Racial Equality (CORE), was arrested for trespassing on school property. Before the police could take him away, however, the assembled demonstrators sat down in front of and behind the police car, preventing it from leaving. Jumping on top of the car, Savio led the rally from there. That evening the demonstrators grappled with policemen to keep the doors of Sproul Hall unlocked while administrators and student representatives negotiated upstairs. On Sproul Hall's steps the situation was just as chaotic, with students, faculty, and school officials arguing about the legitimacy of holding the police car. The demonstration continued until 7:30 the next evening; Weinberg remained in the car the entire time. Even when the crowd dispersed, the battered car was unable to move.

The Free Speech Movement Is Born

On 4 October the demonstrators met again to form an organization to negotiate for them, which they called the Free Speech Movement (FSM). The FSM would be led by the students who had taken the most vocal parts in the capture of the police car. Several months of demonstrations and tense negotiations followed. On 9 November members began setting up tables in the union again, starting another period of open violations of university regulations. As with the first series of demonstrations, hundreds of students volunteered to be punished for the offense. On 20 November the FSM held its largest rally yet, outside where the university's board of regents was meeting to try to resolve what seemed like an increasingly bitter stalemate. Somewhere between 2,000 and 5,000 demonstrators gathered; popular folksinger Joan Baez attended to show her support. The regents' decision was a setback: they voted to pursue new disciplinary action against the eight suspended students and enforce the rules prohibiting political activism on campus more vigorously. When the campus closed for the Thanksgiving holiday, members of the FSM were demoralized: they had been handed a defeat by the regents, and arguments over strategy were starting to jeopardize the movement's solidarity.

On 2 December the FSM held yet another demonstration outside of Sproul Hall; after a series of tense speeches, more than 1,000 students filed into the building. Once inside, they held a free university: faculty members taught classes in languages and civil disobedience, and areas were set aside for sleep, dancing, and watching movies. The sit-in continued well into the night, until more than six hundred police from Berkeley and nearby Oakland arrived to break up the demonstration. They arrested 773 students, who, in classic civil rights style, went limp and had

> Angered by the presence of state police on campus, students and then faculty called for a general strike.

to be carried from the building. The process of removing all the protestors took another twelve hours. Within days, angered by the presence of state police on campus, students and then faculty called for a general strike.

The first day, a Friday, some 10,000 students participated in the strike, cutting classes or picketing the university's gates. Over the weekend the administration decided to negotiate; university president Clark Kerr announced that Monday he would propose a "new era of freedom under law" for the school. Sixteen thousand students packed into an outdoor amphitheater to hear the president's statement. When Savio tried to take the microphone at the end of the meeting, he was wrestled away by two university policemen, and pandemonium resulted. The strike continued into the week; coincidentally, a few days later student elections were held. FSM members and sympathizers received overwhelming support from the student body. On the same day they got another vote of confidence when the faculty senate passed a resolution calling for a lifting of restrictions on political activity on campus. Chancellor Edward Strong was relieved of his duties, and a new chancellor from Berkeley's academic community was chosen as his replacement. For a while it seemed as if the FSM had achieved victory. But that spring protests began again, this time over the use of obscenity in public. The FSM became the "Filthy Speech Movement," and the campus revolts continued.

Photo on previous page: Students stage a "sit-in" at Harvard University during three days of strikes and protests at the school. (Time & Life Pictures/Getty Images.)

Unrest Spread Through Major Universities

Campus unrest was not limited to Berkeley by any means, and particularly after U.S. military involvement in Vietnam intensified in 1965, protests developed across the country. Students and faculty members were increasingly critical of the contributions their schools were making to military research and thus to the war. The draft, understandably of great concern to eighteen-year-old students, prompted scores of hostile demonstrations. At Harvard in 1966 members of the radical group Students for a Democratic Society (SDS) jeered at Defense Secretary Robert McNamara and refused to let his car leave campus; University of Chicago students staged a sit-in to protest Selective Service examinations being held there. In 1967 University of Wisconsin students smashed university property to protest recruitment by Dow Chemical, a major defense contractor, on campus. Student radicals frequently clashed with their more conservative peers and with local authorities, most tragically perhaps at Ohio's Kent State University in May 1970, when the National Guard ended months of tense antiwar protests by shooting into a crowd of demonstrators, killing four and wounding nine others.

Students for a Democratic Society Proclaims Ideals and Goals

Students for a Democratic Society

Students for a Democratic Society (SDS) was an important new leftist group of the 1960s, representing a youthful approach to earlier socialist or Marxist reform efforts. The group held a major meeting in Port Huron, Michigan, on June 11–15, 1962. This convention ratified the results of months of writing and discussion. The lengthy document, known as the Port Huron Statement, became one of the most influential position papers of the 1960s. Its principal writer, Tom Hayden, went on to a famed career of activism as well as elected office in California. The following excerpt includes the beginning and concluding portions of the Port Huron Statement. It summarizes what SDS saw as the urgent needs of America at the time and what should be done about them.

SOURCE. "The Port Huron Statement of the Students for a Democratic Society." New York: Students for a Democratic Society, 1962.

We are people of this generation, bred in at least modest comfort, housed now in universities, looking uncomfortably to the world we inherit. When we were kids the United States was the wealthiest and strongest country in the world: the only one with the atom bomb, the least scarred by modern war, an initiator of the United Nations that we thought would distribute Western influence throughout the world. Freedom and equality for each individual, government of, by, and for the people—these American values we found good, principles by which we could live as men. Many of us began maturing in complacency.

As we grew, however, our comfort was penetrated by events too troubling to dismiss. First, the permeating and victimizing fact of human degradation, symbolized by the Southern struggle against racial bigotry, compelled most of us from silence to activism. Second, the enclosing fact of the Cold War, symbolized by the presence of the Bomb, brought awareness that we ourselves, and our friends, and millions of abstract "others" we knew more directly because of our common peril, might die at any time. We might deliberately ignore, or avoid, or fail to feel all other human problems, but not these two, for these were too immediate and crushing in their impact, too challenging in the demand that we as individuals take the responsibility for encounter and resolution.

While these and other problems either directly oppressed us or rankled our consciences and became our own subjective concerns, we began to see complicated and disturbing paradoxes in our surrounding America. The declaration "all men are created equal" . . . rang hollow before the facts of Negro life in the South and the big cities of the North. The proclaimed peaceful intentions of the United States contradicted its economic and military investments in the Cold War status quo.

We witnessed, and continue to witness, other paradoxes. With nuclear energy whole cities can easily be powered, yet the dominant nationstates seem more likely to unleash destruction greater than that incurred in all wars of human history. Although our own technology is destroying old and creating new forms of social organization, men still tolerate meaningless work and idleness. While two-thirds of mankind suffers undernourishment, our own upper classes revel amidst superfluous abundance. Although world population is expected to double in forty years, the nations still tolerate anarchy as a major principle of international conduct and uncontrolled exploitation governs the sapping of the earth's physical resources. Although mankind desperately needs revolutionary leadership, America rests in national stalemate, its goals ambiguous and tradition-bound instead of informed and clear, its democratic system apathetic and manipulated rather than "of, by, and for the people."

> While two-thirds of mankind suffers undernourishment, our own upper classes revel amidst superfluous abundance.

Not only did tarnish appear on our image of American virtue, not only did disillusion occur when the hypocrisy of American ideals was discovered, but we began to sense that what we had originally seen as the American Golden Age was actually the decline of an era. The worldwide outbreak of revolution against colonialism and imperialism, the entrenchment of totalitarian states, the menace of war, overpopulation, international disorder, supertechnology—these trends were testing the tenacity of our own commitment to democracy and freedom and our abilities to visualize their application to a world in upheaval.

Most Americans Fear Change

Our work is guided by the sense that we may be the last generation in the experiment with living. But we are a minority—the vast majority of our people regard the temporary equilibriums of our society and world as eternally-functional parts. In this is perhaps the outstanding paradox: we ourselves are imbued with urgency, yet the message of our society is that there is no viable alternative to the present. Beneath the reassuring tones of the politicians, beneath the common opinion that America will "muddle through," beneath the stagnation of those who have closed their minds to the future, is the pervading feeling that there simply are no alternatives, that our times have witnessed the exhaustion not only of Utopias, but of any new departures as well. Feeling the press of complexity upon the emptiness of life, people are fearful of the thought that at any moment things might thrust out of control. They fear change itself, since change might smash whatever invisible framework seems to hold back chaos for them now. For most Americans, all crusades are suspect, threatening. The fact that each individual sees apathy in his fellows perpetuates the common reluctance to organize for change. The dominant institutions are complex enough to blunt the minds of their potential critics, and entrenched enough to swiftly dissipate or entirely repel the energies of protest and reform, thus limiting human expectancies. Then, too, we are a materially improved society, and by our own improvements we seem to have weakened the case for further change.

> The ideal university is a community of controversy.

Some would have us believe that Americans feel contentment amidst prosperity—but might it not better be called a glaze above deeply felt anxieties about their role in the new world? And if these anxieties produce a developed indifference to human affairs, do they not as well produce a yearning to believe there is an alternative to the present, that something can be done to change circumstances in the school, the workplaces, the bureaucracies, the government? It is to this latter yearning, at once the spark and engine of change, that we direct our

present appeal. The search for truly democratic alternatives to the present, and a commitment to social experimentation with them, is a worthy and fulfilling human enterprise, one which moves us and, we hope, others today. On such a basis do we offer this document of our convictions and analysis: as an effort in understanding and changing the conditions of humanity in the late twentieth century, an effort rooted in the ancient, still unfulfilled conception of man attaining determining influence over his circumstances of life. . . .

Tom Hayden (third from left), the founder of Students for a Democratic Society, demonstrates his opposition to the Vietnam War when visiting North Vietnam in 1966. (**AP Images.**)

Universities Are Where Change Can Happen

Social relevance, the accessibility to knowledge, and internal openness—these together make the university a potential base and agency in a movement of social change.

1. Any new left in America must be, in large measure, a left with real intellectual skills, committed to deliberativeness, honesty, reflection as working tools. The university permits the political life to be an adjunct to the academic one, and action to be informed by reason.

2. A new left must be distributed in significant social roles throughout the country. The universities are distributed in such a manner.

3. A new left must consist of younger people who matured in the postwar world, and partially be directed to the recruitment of younger people. The university is an obvious beginning point.

4. A new left must include liberals and socialists, the former for their relevance, the latter for their sense of thoroughgoing reforms in the system. The university is a more sensible place than a political party for these two traditions to begin to discuss their differences and look for political synthesis.

5. A new left must start controversy across the land, if national policies and national apathy are to be reversed. The ideal university is a community of controversy, within itself and in its effects on communities beyond.

6. A new left must transform modern complexity into issues that can be understood and felt close-up by every human being. It must give form to the feelings of helplessness and indifference, so that people may see the political, social and economic sources of their

private troubles and organize to change society. In a time of supposed prosperity, moral complacency and political manipulation, a new left cannot rely on only aching stomachs to be the engine force of social reform. The case for change, for alternatives that will involve uncomfortable personal efforts, must be argued as never before. The university is a relevant place for all of these activities.

But we need not indulge in allusions: the university system cannot complete a movement of ordinary people making demands for a better life. From its schools and colleges across the nation, a militant left might awaken its allies, and by beginning the process towards peace, civil rights, and labor struggles, reinsert theory and idealism where too often reign confusion and political barter. The power of students and faculty united is not only potential; it has shown its actuality in the South, and in the reform movements of the North.

The bridge to political power, though, will be built through genuine cooperation, locally, nationally, and internationally, between a new left of young people, and an awakening community of allies. In each community we must look within the university and act with confidence that we can be powerful, but we must look outwards to the less exotic but more lasting struggles for justice.

To turn these possibilities into realities will involve national efforts at university reform by an alliance of students and faculty. They must wrest control of the educational process from the administrative bureaucracy. They must make fraternal and functional contact with allies in labor, civil rights, and other liberal forces outside the campus. They must import major public issues into the curriculum—research and teaching on problems of war and peace is an outstanding example. They must make debate and controversy, not dull pedantic cant, the common style for educational life. They must consciously build a base for their assault upon the loci of power.

As students, for a democratic society, we are committed to stimulating this kind of social movement, this kind of vision and program in campus and community across the country. If we appear to seek the unattainable, it has been said, then let it be known that we do so to avoid the unimaginable.

The President Explains Why Young Americans Must Fight in Vietnam

Lyndon B. Johnson

The Vietnam War was massively controversial. It originated in the mid-1950s as a small conflict between French forces and the Communist government of North Vietnam. The United States aided the French, and then gradually began sending US troops to Vietnam. Under President Lyndon Johnson, the US involvement grew from several thousand advisers to an all-out ground, sea, and air conflict. Not enough Americans volunteered for the military service, so Johnson ordered monthly draft calls. The resultant unwillingness to serve is the context for the following 1965 press conference transcript, in which Johnson puts forth a justification of the US war effort. Lyndon B. Johnson was the president of the United States from 1963 until 1969.

SOURCE. Lyndon B. Johnson, "We Will Stand in Viet-Nam," press conference statement, July 28, 1965.

My fellow Americans: Not long ago I received a letter from a woman in the Midwest. She wrote,

> Dear Mr. President: In my humble way I am writing to you about the crisis in Viet-Nam. I have a son who is now in Viet-Nam. My husband served in World War II. Our country was at war, but now, this time, it is just something that I don't understand. Why?

Well, I have tried to answer that question dozens of times and more in practically every State in this Union. I have discussed it fully in Baltimore in April, in Washington in May, in San Francisco in June. Let me again, now, discuss it here in the East Room of the White House.

Why must young Americans, born into a land exultant with hope and with golden promise, toil and suffer and sometimes die in such a remote and distant place?

The answer, like the war itself, is not an easy one, but it echoes clearly from the painful lessons of half a century. Three times in my lifetime, in two world wars and in Korea, Americans have gone to far lands to fight for freedom. We have learned at a terrible and brutal cost that retreat does not bring safety and weakness does not bring peace.

> "Retreat does not bring safety and weakness does not bring peace."

It is this lesson that has brought us to Viet-Nam. This is a different kind of war. There are no marching armies or solemn declarations. Some citizens of South Viet-Nam, at times with understandable grievances, have joined in the attack on their own government.

But we must not let this mask the central fact that this is really war. It is guided by North Viet-Nam, and it is spurred by Communist China. Its goal is to conquer the South, to defeat American power, and to extend the Asiatic dominion of communism.

There are great stakes in the balance.

The United States Has No Choice

Most of the non-Communist nations of Asia cannot, by themselves and alone, resist growing might and the grasping ambition of Asian communism.

Our power, therefore, is a very vital shield. If we are driven from the field in Viet-Nam, then no nation can ever again have the same confidence in American protection.

In each land the forces of independence would be considerably weakened and an Asia so threatened by Communist domination would certainly imperil the security of the United States itself.

US president Lyndon Johnson (second from right) and the commander of US forces, General William C. Westmoreland (right), visit troops in Vietnam on Christmas Day 1967. (**AP Images.**)

We did not choose to be the guardians at the gate, but there is no one else.

Nor would surrender in Viet-Nam bring peace, because we learned from Hitler at Munich that success only feeds the appetite of aggression. The battle would be renewed in one country and then another country, bringing with it perhaps even larger and crueler conflict, as we have learned from the lessons of history.

> We are in Viet-Nam to fulfill one of the most solemn pledges of the American nation.

Moreover, we are in Viet-Nam to fulfill one of the most solemn pledges of the American nation. Three Presidents—President [Dwight D.] Eisenhower, President [John F.] Kennedy, and your present President—over 11 years have committed themselves and have promised to help defend this small and valiant nation.

Strengthened by that promise, the people of South Viet-Nam have fought for many long years. Thousands of them have died. Thousands more have been crippled and scarred by war. We just cannot now dishonor our word, or abandon our commitment, or leave those who believed us and who trusted us to the terror and repression and murder that would follow.

This, then, my fellow Americans, is why we are in Viet-Nam.

More Troops Will Join the War

What are our goals in that war-stained land?

First: We intend to convince the Communists that we cannot be defeated by force of arms or by superior power. They are not easily convinced. In recent months they have greatly increased their fighting forces and their attacks and the number of incidents. I have asked the Commanding General, General [William C.] Westmoreland, what more he needs to meet this mounting aggression. He has told me. We will meet his needs.

I have today ordered to Viet-Nam the Air Mobile Division and certain other forces which will raise our fighting strength from 75,000 to 125,000 men almost immediately. Additional forces will be needed later, and they will be sent as requested. This will make it necessary to increase our active fighting forces by raising the monthly draft call from 17,000 over a period of time to 35,000 per month, and for us to step up our campaign for voluntary enlistments.

After this past week of deliberations, I have concluded that it is not essential to order Reserve units into service now. If that necessity should later be indicated, I will give the matter most careful consideration and I will give the country due and adequate notice before taking such action, but only after full preparations.

We have also discussed with the Government of South Viet-Nam lately the steps that we will take to substantially increase their own effort, both on the battlefield and toward reform and progress in the villages. Ambassador [Henry Cabot] Lodge is now formulating a new program to be tested upon his return to that area.

I have directed Secretary [of State Dean] Rusk and Secretary [of Defense Robert] McNamara to be available immediately to the Congress to review with these committees, the appropriate congressional committees,

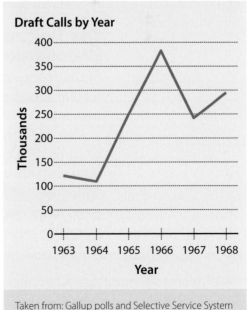

PRESIDENT JOHNSON'S APPROVAL DROPPED AS THE DRAFT GREW

Percentage of Americans Approving of the President

Draft Calls by Year

Taken from: Gallup polls and Selective Service System data.

what we plan to do in these areas. I have asked them to be able to answer the questions of any Member of Congress.

Secretary McNamara, in addition, will ask the Senate Appropriations Committee to add a limited amount to present legislation to help meet part of this new cost until a supplemental measure is ready, and hearings can be held when the Congress assembles in January [1966].

In the meantime, we will use the authority contained in the present defense appropriations bill under consideration, to transfer funds in addition to the additional money that we will ask.

These steps, like our actions in the past, are carefully measured to do what must be done to bring an end to aggression and a peaceful settlement.

We do not want an expanding struggle with consequences that no one can perceive, nor will we bluster or bully or flaunt our power, but we will not surrender and we will not retreat, for behind our American pledge lies the determination and resources, I believe, of all of the American nation.

The United States Welcomes Unconditional Discussions

Second, once the Communists know, as we know, that a violent solution is impossible, then a peaceful solution is inevitable.

We are ready now, as we have always been, to move from the battlefield to the conference table. I have stated publicly and many times, again and again, America's willingness to begin unconditional discussions with any government at any place at any time. Fifteen efforts have been made to start these discussions with the help of 40 nations throughout the world, but there has been no answer.

> We fear the meeting room no more than we fear the battlefield.

But we are going to continue to persist, if persist we must, until death and desolation have led to the same conference table where others could now join us at a much smaller cost.

> We do not seek the destruction of any government, nor do we covet a foot of any territory.

I have spoken many times of our objectives in Viet-Nam. So has the Government of South Viet-Nam. Hanoi has set forth its own proposals. We are ready to discuss their proposals and our proposals and any proposals of any government whose people may be affected, for we fear the meeting room no more than we fear the battlefield.

In this pursuit we welcome and we ask for the concern and the assistance of any nation and all nations. If the United Nations and its officials or any one of its 114 members can by deed or word, private initiative or public action, bring us nearer an honorable peace, then they will have the support and the gratitude of the United States of America.

I have directed [UN] Ambassador [Arthur] Goldberg to go to New York today and to present immediately to Secretary-General U Thant a letter from me requesting that all the resources, energy, and immense prestige of the United Nations be employed to find ways to halt aggression and to bring peace in Viet-Nam.

I made a similar request at San Francisco a few weeks ago, because we do not seek the destruction of any government, nor do we covet a foot of any territory, but we insist and we will always insist that the people of South Viet-Nam shall have the right of choice, the right to shape their own destiny in free elections in the South, or throughout all Viet-Nam under international supervision, and they shall not have any government imposed upon them by force and terror so long as we can prevent it.

This was the purpose of the 1954 agreements which the Communists have now cruelly shattered. If the machinery of those agreements was tragically weak, its purposes still guide our action. As battle rages, we will continue as best we can to help the good people of South Viet-Nam enrich the condition of their life, to feed the hungry, and to tend the sick, and teach the young, and shelter the homeless, and help the farmer to increase crops, and the worker to find a job.

It is an ancient but still terrible irony that while many leaders of men create division in pursuit of grand ambitions, the children of man are really united in the simple, elusive desire for a life of fruitful and rewarding toil.

As I said at Johns Hopkins in Baltimore, I hope that one day we can help all the people of Asia towards that desire. [Presidential adviser] Eugene Black has made great progress since my appearance in Baltimore in that direction—not as the price of peace, for we are ready always to bear a more painful cost, but rather as a part of our obligations of justice toward our fellow man.

A Personal Note

Let me also add now a personal note. I do not find it easy to send the flower of our youth, our finest young men, into battle. I have spoken to you today of the divisions and the forces and the battalions and the units.

But I know them all, every one. I have seen them in a thousand streets, of a hundred towns, in every State in this Union—working and laughing and building, and filled with hope and life. I think that I know, too, how their mothers weep and how their families sorrow. This is the most agonizing and the most painful duty of your President.

There is something else, too. When I was young, poverty was so common that we didn't know it had a name. And education was something that you had to fight for. Water was really life itself. I have now been in public life 35 years, more than three decades, and in each of those 35 years I have seen good men and wise leaders struggle to bring the blessings of this land to all of our people.

Now I am the President. It is now my opportunity to help every child get an education, to help every Negro and every other American citizen have an equal opportunity, to help every family get a decent home, and to help bring healing to the sick and dignity to the old.

As I have said before, that is what I have lived for. That is what I have wanted all my life, since I was a little boy, and I do not want to see all those hopes and all those dreams of so many people for so many years drowned in the wasteful ravages of cruel wars. I am going to do all I can to see that that never happens.

But I also know, as a realistic public servant, that as long as there are men who hate and destroy, we must have the courage to resist or we will see it all—all that we have built, all that we hope to build, all of our dreams for freedom—all—all—will be swept away with the flood of conquest.

So, too, this shall not happen. We will stand in Viet-Nam.

Student Resistance in the 1960s

Mark Edelman Boren

In the 1960s, protests and other dissident actions by students took place around the globe. The following viewpoint summarizes the significant anti-government student activism that took place in Germany and France. The account details the main points of student resistance in Germany, where the official response went so far as to commit murder, and in France, where extensive student actions achieved, for a time at least, solidarity with the working class. The author of several books and numerous other works, Mark Edelman Boren taught English at the University of North Carolina at Wilmington.

SOURCE. Mark Edelman Boren, "Student Resistance in the 1960s," *Student Resistance: A History of the Unruly Subject,* pp. 132–135, 149–154. New York and London: Routledge, 2001. Reproduced by permission.

German Students Go Radical in the 1960s

The first major acts of German student resistance in the 1960s occurred at the Free University in 1965. Students wanted Erich Kuby, a journalist and outspoken critic, to address a commemorative ceremony of the Allied victory over Germany. Outraged by their selection, the university rejected the students' choice. Upset, the students of the Free University turned out for a massive protest against the administration's actions. The administration upset the students yet again when it dismissed an instructor who had attacked the university in a local newspaper. Following the action, thousands of students took to the streets, holding demonstrations and marches and staging strikes for months, and thousands more signed petitions against the administration calling for reform. Although the student protests pressured limited reforms out of the administration, students also were punished for their actions, forbidden by the university to hold political meetings on campus. Incensed at yet another infringement on their freedom of expression, students held large demonstrations that eventually forced the revocation of the new policy. Other assaults on the rights of university students at the Free University met with similar protests.

German students had concerns apart from their own rights and liberties, and the anti-oppression demonstrations blended with anti-imperialist protests. As the government continued to support domestic and international policies that students perceived as oppressive, their resistance increased. Protests against the Vietnam War generated violent clashes with German police, and students perceived the government's turn to physical force as justification for their own; in 1968 and 1969 student groups would increasingly resort to violence to resist their government and the war.

One massive demonstration in June 1967 united those agitating for student rights, those fighting the state's international policies, and those protesting against Iranian persecution of political dissidents, but it also ended up galvanizing student opposition throughout Germany. The shah was touring Berlin, and massive numbers of students converged on the Berlin Opera House, where he was to see a performance. A police line guarded the entrance and secured the shah's safe arrival, and while students were focused on the shah's motorcade, police flanked the demonstrators. With the shah safely inside, authorities ordered the police troops to attack the demonstrators, and they did so—at once and from all sides. The students were overwhelmed, yet the police continued to hit the demonstrators even after it was clear the officers controlled the area. Students, bystanders, even medical personnel trying to rescue the injured were clubbed.

Police kicked one student unconscious, and while they dragged the comatose Benno Ohnesorg to a police wagon, another officer put a gun to the student's head and shot him. The brutal murder provided a cause and a martyr for the student movement. Tens of thousands of students gathered for Ohnesorg's memorial service and a massive protest for university and political reform. They drafted a general statement on the dire need for radical reform to both higher education and the state government.

> In 1968 and 1969 student groups would increasingly resort to violence.

Rudi Dutschke (popularly known as "Red Rudi") led the students in their resolution and the movement it engendered. In addition to blaming the government and the undemocratic university system for programmatically suppressing students' rights, Dutschke identified an enemy for the cause . . . directing the students' anger toward a chain of newspapers owned by Axel Springer that distorted the public's view of students. In a move reminiscent of medieval universities, radical students also created the floating Negative University, which had neither buildings nor set curriculum; it offered ad hoc courses centered around strategic resistance. In the spring of 1968 Dutschke was shot and sidelined; students blamed the newspapers for inciting the would-be assassin and began attacking distributors of Springer papers and vandalizing their offices. From 1968 on, radical students increasingly resorted to violence to prevent the distribution of Springer papers, raiding stores and firebombing company offices.

As the 1960s progressed, both German students and police used violence, resulting in paranoia on the part of both sides, with rough arrests leading to violent protests and more arrests. The situation escalated rapidly. In April 1967, for example, police arrested and roughed up eleven student members of the Commune for planning to assassinate U.S. vice president Hubert Humphrey on his trip to Berlin; acting on a tip, police hit the group in a preemptive strike and discovered a large cache of homemade "weapons" made of pudding, yogurt, and smoke bombs. But even if some student resistance actions were prankish, the violent tenor of the student movement was no laughing matter. In December 1967, for example, students protested in a ritzy shopping area of West Berlin just before Christmas, showering holiday shoppers with images of Vietnamese dead and shouting slogans critiquing thoughtless consumption at a time when thousands were being killed due to German indifference to the war in Vietnam. Berlin police reacted swiftly, with enough force and brutality to disperse the marchers almost instantaneously—confirming the students' claims of state oppression as they freed the streets for the holiday. The brutality of police suppression and the government's forceful response to the growing German student movement of the mid-1960s set the stage for the 1968 turmoil to come in Germany by radicalizing student activists and fostering a situation in which student extremists saw violence as the only viable course of action. In 1968 and 1969 student groups launched a terrorist campaign that captured government and media attention, but also discredited the student movement for most of the German public. . . .

1968: The Year of the Student

No year has been written about more in relation to student activism, no year is more mythologized or brings more sighs of melancholic yearning to aging activists, than what has come to be known as the Year of the Student, 1968. From Paris to Tokyo, Mexico City to Dakar, in one single year students staged an unprecedented number of major resistance actions, actions that dramatically changed the course of their respective nations and the world; students all over the globe pushed their individual movements to crisis points as the international media watched, reported, and capitalized on their stories, applauding or condemning the movements' issues, strategies, and heroes. Many of the actions begun in 1968 continued in 1969 (and indeed, some of the most important effects of 1968 student actions weren't felt until the 1970s), but as for a historical moment that crystallized the global power of the student—1968 is it.

The Year of the Student and the Students of France

In January a group of students at the University of Paris, Nanterre, calling themselves Les Enragés, or the maniacs, after an extremist group in the French Revolution and borrowing the tactics of the Situationists—an anarchist, antibourgeois, anticapitalist group of antiaesthetic agitators—began creating disturbances on campus, disrupting university lectures, classes, and events. Situationist-inspired slogans—"The more you consume the less you live!" or "I take my desires for reality because

I believe in the reality of my desires!"—began appearing on Nanterre university walls. Les Enragés, composed of highly motivated student radicals and scores of willing followers, extended their disruptions throughout the campus, at first hurling only insults at those whom they perceived as fascist bourgeois professors and speakers, but soon hurling stones as well; they called for immediate educational reforms (co-ed dormitories topped their list of demands), but they also demanded the destruction of imperialism, the military, the bourgeoisie, and the university itself. Situationist propaganda had primed the students of France for action; *On the Poverty of Student Life*, a radical call for insurrection, was first published in 1966 by members of the Situationist International and a group of Strasbourg students, and by 1968 it had circulated throughout France's universities, with over 300,000 copies printed. Although the students took themselves seriously, the Situationists were using them to sow anarchy and using their student union funds to print Situationist pamphlets. Independent Situationist-inspired organizations already existed in schools across the nation by the time Les Enragés students were scaling the entrance to the Nanterre campus at night to hang banners reading, "Never Work!"

From the start, the 1968 student upheavals were an international potlatch of strategies and concerns. In March 1968 Les Enragés seized an administration building at the Nanterre campus to protest the arrest of students suspected in a series of anti-Vietnam War bombings. Led by Daniel ("Danny the Red") Cohn-Bendit, the radical students at Nanterre modeled themselves on Fidel Castro's July Twenty-Sixth Movement, calling their own revolutionary action the March Twenty-Second Movement. They also endeavored

> "From the start, the 1968 student upheavals were an international potlatch of strategies and concerns.

Students clash with police during rioting in Paris on May 6, 1968, after days of strikes and demonstrations against police oppression. (AFP/Getty Images.)

to start an urban revolution as they protested against the Vietnam War, Western imperialism, and militarism. The surprising success of the Tet offensive in Vietnam, the embarrassing defeat of overconfident American forces in an impoverished third-world country, and the growing and highly visible unrest of American students fueled the revolutionary fires of the French radicals, who claimed they would start their own war in France. Hostilities on the campus between the demonstrators and the administration threatened to erupt, and the president of the school temporarily closed the university. Shortly after the school opened again, demonstrations and disruptions again occurred on campus, and the administration reclosed the school, announcing that disciplinary hearings would be held for the Enragés core members on May 6 at the Sorbonne. The radicals had only a few days to prepare for their defense. Instead, they went on the offensive.

Les Enragés met other radical students from the University of Paris at the Sorbonne to address a large crowd of Sorbonne and Nanterre students. When police began arresting those students gathered, Sorbonne students raised an alarm and attacked the police. Provoked, the police charged into the unruly students with clubs, and the entire area erupted in a riot in which hundreds of students and bystanders were injured. The largely unorganized student uprising continued the next day, spreading through Paris and then through the nation as student organizations and unions went on strike and joined the demonstrations against police oppression. By May 5, most of the major student organizations, including the Union Nationale des Etudiants de France, supported an immediate national strike.

On the supposed day of the hearings, May 6, students numbering in the thousands demonstrated on the Boulevard Saint-Michele to protest the violence of May 4 and the police occupation of the Sorbonne. In spite of massive Parisian public support (the numbers swelled as the march continued), the police brutally attacked the demonstrators as they approached the Sorbonne. This time the students refused to run, and when the police fired tear gas grenades, the protesters covered their faces with wet rags; they organized themselves into long columns, passing bricks and paving stones torn up from streets blocks away up to front lines of students facing off with police. The students continued the assault for over seven hours, until police troop reinforcements finally overwhelmed them in a concerted push. The entire quarter became the scene of rioters and police run amok; students, onlookers, residents, emergency health workers—police attacked them all. . . . Groups of students and police officers fought each other throughout the night. Relying on urban guerilla tactics—many of them Blanquist—the students had, in a fashion, started their own war on the Left Bank after all.

On May 7, the Union Nationale des Etudiants de France held a massive demonstration on the Champs Elysées; forty thousand students attended—the Arc de Triomphe floated in a sea of waving banners. Over the next few days students in each of France's major cities held huge demonstrations, demanding the release of arrested students and protesters, the recall of police presence from universities, and a gamut of educational and social reforms. . . . Even though the protesting groups often professed disparate beliefs, and the relations between then were sometimes strained, Communists and hard-line Trotskyists marched together with anarchists and Situationists, united in opposing the Gaullist government and the brutality of French riot police. For several days students and police waged battles in the streets of the Left Bank.

By May 10 tens of thousands of students had taken over the Left Bank, where they fashioned barricades in the streets out of furniture, cars, bricks, bicycles, and anything and everything that they could carry and stack. The demonstration was by and large leaderless; and although the lack of centralized control diluted the protest's power, it also made suppression of the students difficult. Supporters continued to mass, and by nightfall the streets swarmed with thousands of demonstrators armed with stones, bottles, bricks, Molotov cocktails, and whatever they could use as missiles, bombs, or clubs, standing on or behind massive barricades. The upcoming fight in many ways was unavoidable. De Gaulle's government was damned if they attacked the barricades and damned if they didn't; to attack would cast the police once again as the brutal oppressors, while to delay would be to appear weak. De Gaulle was not one to back down, and early in the morning of May 11 thousands of police troops charged the barricades. The clash of sticks, the thuds of truncheons, the clattering of thrown stones, the explosions of gas tanks, the firing and hiss of tear gas canisters, and yells and moans filled the streets of Paris. After intense fighting, the students were thrown off their fortifications, and many discovered too late that they had neglected to provide themselves with escape routes. Police beat protesters, even storming apartments suspected of harboring them. Many terrified and pleading protesters found sanctuary and protection in the homes of sympathetic residents, but a great many did not. For the remainder of the night, students skirmished with police troops throughout the Latin Quarter.

The French government tried to defuse the situation by withdrawing troops from university campuses, but the revolt by then had too much momentum to be diverted; workers' unions announced their own general strikes for May 13, the tenth anniversary of de Gaulle's ascension to power, and the workers brought their own demands to the protest. Workers at major industrial plants occupied their factories or joined in public demonstrations; suddenly millions of French factory workers were striking. Public service, shipyard, and other workers joined the strike—all with their own demands for government or labor reform. France's workers had grown increasingly upset at rising work demands, the lowest wages in industrialized Europe, and a growing national unemployment rate. The government's economic policies had slowly pushed blue-collar workers to a flash point: the Paris student riots simply ignited the flame. In an effort to consolidate power, many student groups marched to factories to establish relations

> "Suddenly millions of French factory workers were striking.

between striking laborers and students. As Paris erupted in riots, and industrial France ground to a halt, de Gaulle found his grip on the country in serious jeopardy. The French workers offered the more dangerous threat to the government, but the students kept Paris on the edge of revolution. . . . Les Enragés and the Situationists officially joined forces, and the two groups continued to try to radicalize the exploding student movement. The core group of students at the Sorbonne, however, were no longer in control of the student uprising, nor would the studentry adopt the increasingly militant stances of the radicals, who now sought de Gaulle's overthrow. Frustrated with the general student masses, who no longer listened to them, Les Enragés and the Situationists abandoned the Sorbonne to the students.

The division between the radical learners, the more moderate masses, and those students simply rioting for the sake of it spoke to other fractures in the tenuous coalition of resistance. The protesting students could not agree among themselves on their goals, while the workers wanted concrete economic reforms and wage increases. Trouble soon plagued this partnership as well, as the laborers perceived the students as irresponsible, too radical, and unpredictable.

> The general public had grown frustrated with the students' abuse of property, their general disorganization, and their radicalness.

Nevertheless, by May 27, de Gaulle's government's demise seemed imminent. Students kept protesting, and labor unions held out for wage increases and other reforms. The seventy-seven-year-old president abruptly left Paris at the end of May. His departure stunned the populace of Paris, and students claimed victory; but the aged war veteran was determining if he still enjoyed the support of the military, and he did. One day later he returned to Paris to give a public radio speech in which he called for national elections. After de Gaulle's speech, a spontaneous rally of hundreds of thousands of his supporters marched down the Champs Elysées waving French flags and intoning the "Marseillaise." By this time the general public had grown frustrated with the students' abuse of property, their general disorganization, and their radicalness; urban residents also began to feel the strain of the interruption of daily life and of social services (public transportation had long since been discontinued, and the cities had run nearly, if not completely, out of gasoline). De Gaulle's first decisive move of his new campaign came on June 1, when he had all the gasoline stations restocked with fuel for the long Whitsun weekend; traffic once again flowed in Paris, and the tide of fortune turned against the students and workers as the general public began to appreciate a society that worked. Strikers at factories tried to hold out against the reenergized regime but eventually succumbed to police troops, and the police overran the Sorbonne early in June. On June 23 the Gaullist government swept the elections, and immediately instituted educational reforms and a wage increase, which satisfied students and workers enough to return the majority of them to their former employments. By the end of the month de Gaulle was once again securely in power, and students were once again sitting at their desks.

> Although the students and the workers of France pushed the Gaullist regime to the brink of disaster, they lacked the leadership and the political power to topple it.

Thus although the students and the workers of France pushed the Gaullist regime to the brink of disaster, they lacked the leadership and the political power to topple it. When both movements stalled, de Gaulle was able to rally his political and police forces against them. Satisfied the military backed him, de Gaulle used his political power to call elections, relying on nonurban popular support and frustrated city residents who had grown impatient with the protests and the interruptions to daily life and of public service. The students and workers generated enough power to threaten de Gaulle's regime, but they were unable to focus it effectively and decisively.

High School Activism Started Later but Was Widespread

Gael Graham

By the late 1960s, events of unrest or protest were reported at almost half of American high schools, according to the following viewpoint by history professor Gael Graham. While racial issues were especially divisive, dress code protests were more prevalent, she notes. Student journalists fought censorship. Students in general cited hypocrisy within school administrations and in society, and wanted to participate in ending it, Graham asserts. Graham is an associate professor of history and the director of the History Graduate Program at Western Carolina University.

S tudent activism, although forgotten or minimized today, seriously disrupted many American high schools. Beginning somewhat later than college

---

SOURCE. Gael Graham, *Young Activists: American High School Students in the Age of Protest.* DeKalb: Northern Illinois University Press, 2006, pp. 5–9. Used with permission of Northern Illinois University Press. All rights reserved. Reproduced by permission.

activism, high school activism peaked between 1968 and 1973, when the college movement was already ebbing. One widely cited 1969 survey published by the National Association of Secondary School Principals reported unrest in 59 percent of responding high schools and 56 percent of junior high schools. More astonishingly, more than half of the rural schools had experienced disruptions. The House Subcommittee on General Education conducted a national survey of all twenty-nine thousand public and private schools in 1968, finding disturbances in 18 percent; the following year, the number soared to 40 percent. Researchers emphasized that they tabulated instances of significant, disruptive, and collective student action, not individual disciplinary problems. Because there were many more high schools than there were colleges and universities, these findings indicate a startling degree of turbulence. In addition to general unrest, more than two dozen schools reported bombings and attempted bombings in 1969 alone. These figures may appear exaggerated, but in fact they probably underestimate the actual degree of disruption, because researchers typically either polled school officials, many of whom did not respond or downplayed events at their school, or counted newspaper stories about high school unrest. Nor is it always clear what was being counted. The terms "unrest" and "protest" suggest both mindless mayhem and purposeful student actions: both are accurate. Some schools essentially experienced race riots—violence devoid of specific political content other than racial hatred. In other cases, student disruptions aimed at obtaining well-articulated demands.

Many Issues Concerned High School Students

Confirming the widespread occurrence of high school activism and dissidence raises a number of questions. What caused these students to protest? What forms did their activism take? Did they merely mimic college activists? How did school officials, parents, local communities, and government respond to high school dissent?

Every issue that concerned college students engaged some high school students as well. Racial integration, for example, was particularly divisive. School districts and local administrators mandated desegregation, often under compulsion

> Every issue that concerned college students engaged some high school students as well.

from federal courts, but those in the schools, including students, carried it out and contested the nitty-gritty details. Black, Latino, and white students jostled each other in the halls, bathrooms, and cafeterias, and they fought bitterly over ownership of and access to social space at dances, athletic events, pep rallies, and student clubs. Seemingly trivial issues such as the selection of cheerleaders or homecoming court members sparked furious explosions because many whites believed that compulsory integration required only chilly toleration of the newcomers' presence; they did not intend to incorporate minority students into the fabric of school life, let alone reweave that fabric into a new pattern. But as Black and Brown Power ideologies surged into public high schools in the late 1960s, students of color seized the initiative, hacking out their own racialized spaces through demands for representation among teachers and administrators, a restructured curricula that would celebrate their history and culture, and even the spice of their own food in the cafeteria. Taking to the streets, both Latino and African-American students counted on the support of older community members in their battles with white students and officials. Ironically, many whites objected to separatist school organizations although they had not previously protested all-white school activities or clubs.

Dress Codes Were Inflammatory

If protests against dress codes caused less violence than race relations, they did outnumber racial confrontations. Regulations about hair length and style for boys, skirt length or pants for girls, shirts tucked in or pulled out, armbands, and political buttons prompted fiery debates in schools and communities. Students were by no means united in opposing dress and hair codes. Some student councils drew up codes that embodied the official view that neat attire promoted good attitudes, academic achievement, and school pride. Other students, particularly athletes, acted as unofficial enforcers for dress codes, especially strictures against long hair for boys. Although some students resisted dress codes as individuals or sued their schools, others protested collectively. Punishments for dress code violations and principals' vetoes of more lenient codes passed by student councils in turn led to new debates about student power and the effectiveness of student governance.

The First Amendment Rights Were Expanded

Similarly, the blossoming of unofficial underground newspapers and battles over censorship of school newspapers raised questions about the rights of high school students. Here, too, surprising numbers of students filed lawsuits, in a period when the courts vigilantly protected and expanded First Amendment rights. For other students, disputes over both fashions and substantive rights exposed the arbitrary power of school officials and the powerlessness of students. This insight propelled them to wage war over more fundamental issues such as the proper relationship between students and educators, and many students demanded that officials accept them as partners in education.

Those who attacked the status quo in the 1960s did not propose novelty for its own sake; in most cases, they

On the signs:

DOES SOCIETY HANG BY A HAIR?

JESUS SHAKESPEARE WASHINGTON LINCOLN.... WORE LONG HAIR WHO SHOULD WE LOOK UP TO?

IT'S NOT THE HAIR ON TOP BUT THE MIND UNDERNEATH

IT'S 1968 NOT 1984

BEETHOVEN IN A CREWCUT?

called attention to the gap between rhetoric and reality. African-Americans and Latinos exposed white hypocrisy in publicly affirming a creed of equality while maintaining racial apartheid and discrimination; the Kinsey report [on sexuality] showed how little official morality meant behind closed doors, and antiwar protesters emphasized both how poorly the term "free Vietnam" fit the unpopular, repressive government of the South and how the American manner of waging war undercut the values the war was intended to protect. Similarly, high school students perceived multiple divergences between rhetoric and reality, both in society and within the high schools themselves. Some argued, in fact, that the flaws in American society were the flaws in its high schools writ large.

Students in Norwalk, Connecticut, protest their high school's restrictions on beards and hair length in January 1968. (Copyright Bettmann/Corbis/AP Images.)

Young Students Took a Challenge to School—and to Court

A notable example of quiet activism by young students took place in Des Moines, Iowa, in December of 1965. To protest the Vietnam War, a group of students decided to wear black armbands to their high schools and junior highs from December 16 until New Year's Day.

School principals learned of the plan and, on December 14, declared that any student wearing such an armband would be suspended. Fearing harm to their educational futures, most of the students backed down. Of the more than two dozen who persisted, a few were singled out for discipline, including John Tinker, fifteen, his sister Mary Beth, thirteen, and Christopher Eckhardt, sixteen.

With the support of their parents, the three took the school system to court.

The case, known as *Tinker v. Des Moines School District*, ultimately went to the US Supreme Court. The court ruled on February 24, 1969, in favor of the students, finding they had a First Amendment right to express opinions and had done so in a way that was not disruptive nor impinging on the rights of others. Because the students did not interfere with school operations, the schools had no right to prohibit the armbands, the Court said. The ruling was a landmark regarding the rights of students in public schools.

Authority Was Challenged

Beyond questioning the status quo and exposing some of the lies Americans told themselves, activists in the 1960s—including high school students—challenged public and private authorities. Although adolescents typically challenge authority, this is usually fought out between individual youths and the authorities in their lives. What is noteworthy in the 1960s is that high school students organized, laid out their reasons for opposing the rules that bound them, using both the language of rights and revolution, and suggested alternative ways of running schools and society. Most collective efforts centered on a single high school, but students in a number of cities created citywide high school student organizations, and several groups attempted (briefly) to create a national high school news network in the late 1960s.

> The term 'participation' sums up the overarching demand of activist high school students.

As was the case with many other groups in the 1960s, the term "participation" sums up the overarching demand of activist high school students in this era. African-American and other minority students wanted to participate fully in school and society; they also wanted their contributions and heritage recognized and valued. Even when they rejected participation in white-dominated school and society, they demanded the right to create alternative spaces of their own. Participation also meant having a hand in running the schools. Most student activists of all races accepted the necessity of formal education. They were not seeking to outlaw school itself, but they objected to the absence of any student voice in determining what they should learn, how they should learn it, what rules they should follow, and what consequences there should be for failure to comply.

When high school students analyzed their schools in terms of power relations, they often perceived links between high school politics and the wider society. These students wanted debates about the war in Vietnam, civil rights, Black Power, dissident politics, and, to a lesser extent, feminism and environmentalism brought into the schools, both in the classroom and through outside speakers and student clubs. Although they often couched their demands in terms of balancing the conservative agendas of school officials, these students were unambiguously and self-consciously left wing, calling themselves "liberals" or "radicals."

Just as many southern whites believed that "their Negroes" had been content under Jim Crow law before civil rights "outsiders" came to town, many adults insisted that without outside agitation high school activism would not have developed. The temper of the times greatly influenced high school activists, providing them with a language to speak, methods to borrow, and evidence that agitation worked. In these ways, we can see that high school activism did not occur in a historical vacuum, for all of the social and political movements of the era fed each other, contributing to the heady sense of possibility that many activists felt.

The influence of college activism is more difficult to gauge. Extensive media coverage guaranteed that most high school students knew about events taking place on the campuses. Some doubtless had friends or siblings in college. Moreover, beginning in 1969 the best-known college activist group, Students for a Democratic Society (SDS), actively recruited high school students and established a number of high school SDS chapters. But as SDS degenerated into the Weather Underground in the late 1960s, plans to recruit younger students as revolutionaries came to naught. The latter resented college students trying to tell them what to do and rebuffed organizers who seemed out of touch with their needs.

Young Activists Set Their Own Paths

High school activists did resemble college activists in some ways: they were a minority, they were among the brightest and most articulate students, they tended to share rather than oppose the political beliefs of their parents, whose support they generally enjoyed, and most—though not all—tried working first through "proper channels." Other students were not activists in any sustained sense but could be mobilized to protest specific, usually local, grievances. This latter group cut across student types in terms of race, class, and academic achievement.

Despite their similarities, high school student activists were neither pawns nor mere imitators of older dissidents. They generally maintained their distance from college activists.

> High school student activists were neither pawns nor mere imitators of older dissidents.

Moreover, activists were often awakened in high school, contradicting the belief that influence flowed from older to younger students. In one attempt to predict future college unrest, three professors polled incoming college freshmen from 1966 to 1969 and tracked those who had participated in high school protests. They found that in 1969, as part of a rising curve, about 12 percent had protested U.S. military policy, 20 percent had demanded changes in race relations, and more than 45 percent had challenged high school rules. But researchers ignored the implications of this for high schools, concentrating instead on how many of these students might become protesters in college. Here is a clear instance of high school students potentially bringing their activism to college, rather than the dynamic working the other way. Similarly, one teacher revealed in a 1983 interview that her activism originated during her high school days in the 1960s, when she had lobbied Congress to support school desegregation. After she started college, she found it a "very easy transition" to organize full-time for SDS.

School and government officials and educational experts disagreed on how to handle high school unrest. Many school officials treated dissident students as discipline problems, whereas outside authorities—who did not have to deal with these students on a daily basis—counseled concessions to student demands. Even when these experts advised against concessions, they proposed the creation of a mechanism through which students could express their grievances. While some high school principals and school board members drew up plans calling for police intervention, professional educational journals recommended setting up student advisory groups and appointing ombudsmen to keep open communications between students and the administration. Educational experts also supported demands for a more up-to-date curriculum, more choice of electives, and greater variety in teaching methods.

High school dissidence in the late 1960s and early 1970s was thus a widespread, highly visible, and much-discussed problem. Adults even feared that it might ultimately prove more disruptive than college demonstrations. At the beginning of the 1970–1971 school year, for example, the superintendent of schools in El Paso, Texas, dramatically warned officials to brace themselves for more "student strikes and demonstrations than ever before in history."

CHAPTER 2

Controversies Surrounding Student Movements of the 1960s

Communists Duped Youths and Threatened the United States from Within

US House Committee on Un-American Activities

J. Edgar Hoover, the longtime director of the Federal Bureau of Investigation, was an ardent anti-Communist. He found a more than supportive audience in the US House of Representatives when he reported to that body's Committee on Un-American Activities. The following viewpoint, excerpted from the committee's annual report for 1960, conveys Hoover's conviction that the first wave of student activism was guided by Communists and was a grave threat to the United States. He focuses on a set of hearings that took place in San Francisco in May of 1960, hearings that evolved into chaos and violence. The US House Committee on Un-American Activities was established in 1938 and abolished in 1975.

SOURCE. US House Committee on Un-American Activities, "Communist Target—Youth," *Annual Report for the Year 1960*, pp. 77–82. Washington: US Government Printing Office, 1961.

The student riots against the Committee on Un-American Activities [HCUA] in San Francisco, California, May 13, 1960, were Communist-inspired and Communist-incited. This was the report of J. Edgar Hoover, Director of the Federal Bureau of Investigation, to the committee. Mr. Hoover said that the riots were termed "the most successful Communist coup to occur in the San Francisco area in 25 years" by experienced West Coast observers familiar with Communist strategy and tactics. . . .

In line with a long-standing party aim to destroy not only the Committee on Un-American Activities, but also the Senate Internal Security Subcommittee, the Communist Party had reaffirmed its dedication to "abolish" these two investigative committees in a resolution adopted at its 17th National Convention in December 1959.

Thus, according to Mr. Hoover, when the decision of the Committee on Un-American Activities, to hold hearings May 12–14, 1960, in San Francisco was announced, it was mandatory for Communists to implement the convention resolution by "doing everything possible to disrupt the hearings as part of the overall aim to destroy the HCUA." . . .

Two Stages of Attack

For the 1960 hearings, the Communists planned two stages of attack. The first was to pack the hearings with demonstrators. The second was to incite these demonstrators to "action" through the use of mob psychology.

In organizing the first stage of attack, the Communist Party decided to build support around one of the subpenaed witnesses, Douglas Wachter, an 18-year-old sophomore at the University of California who had attended the Seventeenth National Convention of the Communist Party. According to Mr. Hoover, Douglas Wachter proceeded to organize student demonstrators on his campus immediately after he had been served with a subpoena.

Roscoe Proctor, a member of the district committee of the Northern California District of the Communist Party, was instructed by the district chairman, Mickey Lima, to contact additional students at the University of California and enlist their support. Lima was also assured that student support would be forthcoming from Santa Rosa Junior College and San Francisco State College.

> A circular to all Communists in the San Francisco area outlined the plan of attack.

A circular to all Communists in the San Francisco area outlined the plan of attack, and rank-and-file party members quickly responded.

Party members immediately circulated petitions, published protest advertisements, initiated fund drives, and arranged for radio broadcasts to stimulate resistance to the Committee on Un-American Activities.

A party telephone campaign, designed specifically to reach 1,000 people, solidified party action. Mr. Hoover pointed out that Merle Brodsky, an active leader of the Communist Party in California for 20 years, "boasted that he was calling everyone he had ever known enlisting support for the demonstrations."

Mr. Hoover added that a simultaneous campaign was initiated by various Communist-controlled groups in the area, including the Citizens Committee to Preserve American Freedoms and the East Bay Community Forum. These organizations, financially assisted by the Communist Party, circulated literature opposing the committee and calling for its abolition. Mr. Hoover added:

> As the scheduled time for the hearings neared, Communists stepped up their efforts to assure a big turnout. Communist leaders in Berkeley arranged transportation from Berkeley to San Francisco for youths interested

in attending each of the 3-day hearings. Meetings were held; leaflets appeared on campuses; and telephone calls were made with increasing urgency. By May 11, 1960, party leaders knew they had succeeded in the first stage of their planned campaign. . . . Demonstrators would be out in full force.

San Francisco police use hoses on demonstrators protesting the House Committee on Un-American Activities hearings in 1960. (Copyright Bettmann/Corbis/AP Images.)

Provocative Outbursts Were Planned

Simultaneously, the party initiated plans to carry out the second stage of their planned attack. Mr. Hoover quoted one of the subpoenaed witnesses, Saul Wachter, as saying to party members that the committee would encounter "plenty of opposition" and that demonstrations would be staged against the committee.

He added that Archie Brown, a former member of the party's National Committee, and Merle Brodsky planned physical outbursts during the hearings "so that they would be forcibly ejected and thus enabled to play on the sympathies of the students."

Party officials gave explicit orders to various witnesses as to how to behave before the committee. Mr. Hoover revealed that on May 6, 1960, Mickey Lima told party members he had met with Leibel Bergman, Andy Negro, and Vern Bown to insure that they would be hostile witnesses.

In addition, the party intended to have an approved document read into the record for future party use by Juanita Wheeler, another subpoenaed party member.

Final arrangements included the distribution of additional pamphlets, preparation of posters and placards for the demonstrators to carry, and a party-sponsored "Peace March" on Saturday, May 14, 1960, at the conclusion of the hearings.

Mr. Hoover stated that the well-organized plan of attack unfolded according to schedule as the hearings began. Archie Brown and Merle Brodsky were so contemptuous in their behavior inside the hearing room that they were forcibly ejected. Mr. Hoover continued:

> An organized clique of sympathizers in the hearing room aided them in their roles. . . . Approximately 25 percent of the spectators in the room were individuals under subpoena and their relatives, friends, attorneys, and sympathizers.

These people provided vocal support for the 36 uncooperative witnesses as they unleashed their bitter attacks against the committee during interrogation.

Mr. Hoover added that during the luncheon recess on May 12, Brown and Brodsky again incited a demonstration inside the hearing room.

They seized a microphone and demanded that all spectators outside the room be admitted. This received the support of the sympathetic clique within the room, and finally Brown, Brodsky, and several others had to be forcibly ejected from the room when they refused to obey orders to be seated.

Mr. Hoover added:

> Brown's plan to incite the crowd was beginning to materialize. Upon his ejection from the hearing room, sympathetic cheers went up from the crowd, consisting mostly of students, gathered inside City Hall at the head of the staircase leading to the room.

The Second-Day Crowd Was Bigger

Although police were able, for the most part, to maintain law and order on the first day of the hearings, a larger crowd appeared on the scene the second day.

Mr. Hoover stated,

> A particularly noticeable aspect of the increase was the presence of additional party members and former party members.

A municipal court judge in the City Hall ordered that the building be cleared because the noisy demonstrators made it impossible for him to hold court. When police officials attempted to enforce this judicial ruling, the crowds responded by "throwing shoes and jostling the officers," according to Mr. Hoover's report.

Police warned the mob that fire hoses would be turned on if it did not disperse in obedience to the judge's order. The mob, instigated by strategically placed Communists, refused to move.

According to Mr. Hoover's report:

> One of the demonstrators provided the spark that touched off the flame of violence. Leaping a barricade that had been erected, he grabbed an officer's night stick and began beating the officer over the head. The mob

Congressmen Heard a Strongly Worded Dissent

When a committee of the US House of Representatives scheduled a set of hearings in San Francisco in 1960, it set the stage for the first major protest of the 1960s. The House Un-American Activities Committee wanted to root out and condemn what it saw as subversive individuals and groups. A countervailing opinion was that the committee was trampling on freedom of speech and other rights of a democracy.

The hearings opened May 13, 1960. Ordered to appear before the congressmen were university faculty members, at least one student, writers, political organizers, and others. The hearings quickly turned confrontational. An example from the government transcript:

> Richard Arens, committee counsel: "Are you now or have you ever been a member of the Communist Party?"

> William Mandel, researcher and teacher: ". . . If you think that I am going to cooperate with this collection of Judases, of men who sit there in violation of the United States Constitution, if you think I will cooperate with you in any way, you are insane!"

Outside the hearing room, police clashed with protesting students, injuring dozens and arresting sixty-eight. More days of clashes followed; the foundation was laid for the Free Speech Movement in nearby Berkeley.

surged forward as if to storm the doors, and a Police Inspector ordered the fire hose turned on. The water forced the crowd to the head of the balustrade, and the cold water had a sobering effect on the emotions of the demonstrators.

During a brief lull in the rioting, police officers removed some of the resisting demonstrators from the building. "Suddenly, realizing what was happening, militant individuals in the group set the pattern for renewed violence by kicking and striking the officers."

The third day of the hearings, Mr. Hoover reported, saw more threatened violence, as a crowd of about 2,000 gathered at the scene. A party attorney from Oakland, Bertram Edises, incited further resistance to the committee when he became so arrogant and insulting in his appearance as a witness before the committee that he had to be removed from the hearing room.

Committee members were escorted out of the building as the suddenly aroused crowd surged toward the entrance of City Hall and toward policemen assigned to maintain law and order.

The Communists Loved the Riot

In evaluating the demonstrations and riots against the Committee on Un-American Activities, Mr. Hoover stated:

> The Communist Party, USA, is elated with the success it enjoyed in attempting to make a fiasco of the HCUA San Francisco hearings, which, notwithstanding these attempts at disruption, did develop valuable and needed information concerning the strategy, tactics, and activities of the party in northern California.

Several factors pleased the party particularly. First, the number of students that the Communists had been able to recruit for "action." Secondly, the number of former party members the affair had brought back into the ranks of the party. Thirdly, the beneficial effect the demonstrations had had upon various Communist functions, such as a fund drive for the party's West Coast publication, *People's World*, which reportedly received much supporting mail from individuals throughout the United States and the world.

Mr. Hoover wrote:

> In short the consensus in the Communist Party was that the riot was the best thing for the party that had occurred in years. . . . The feeling was that not only had the party taken a major step toward its goal of abolishing the HCUA, but also it had taken a major step toward playing a greater role on the American scene.

Following the riots, the party decided to keep its campaign active. In an attempt to rally further student support, Archie Brown announced on May 20, 1960, that the party planned to emphasize "police brutality" to attract the sympathy of student groups. Brown was subsequently invited, along with other Communist leaders, to address youth groups and students at colleges in the San Francisco area. Further exploitation of youth in the area was anticipated by the party as it prepared to distribute 20,000 leaflets, captioned "From Blackmail to Blackjack," on college campuses.

In concluding his report, F.B.I. Director Hoover warned that the Communists in San Francisco proved just how powerful a weapon Communist infiltration is: "They revealed how it is possible for only a few Communist agitators, using mob psychology, to turn peaceful demonstrations into riots."

> "Mr. Hoover concluded by emphasizing the importance which youth plays in the future of this country."

Mr. Hoover concluded by emphasizing the importance which youth plays in the future of this country. Although the vast majority of American youth has demonstrated that it deserves "our confidence and support," the Communist conspiracy has also demonstrated that its efforts to infiltrate youth and student groups, labor unions, churches, professional groups, artists, newspapers, government, and the like, can "create chaos and shatter our internal security."

Mr. Hoover mentioned that today governments are toppling with "stunning rapidity" and warned:

> Whether large or small, the role Communists are playing in these events must not be discounted. The growing strength of our Nation over the years has not proven a deterrent to relentless efforts on the part of the Communist Party, USA, to destroy our security and prepare our Nation for a similar fate.
>
> Looking at the riots and chaos Communists have created in other countries, many Americans point to the strength of our Nation and say "It can't happen here." The Communist success in San Francisco in May 1960 proves that it can happen here.

Southern Black College Students Endured Great Risks Through Nonviolent Protest

Jeffrey A. Turner

In the early 1960s, black college students in the southern United States were a minority of a minority. So, when some decided to challenge racial discrimination, they took a frightening risk, according to history teacher Jeffrey Turner. He details the profoundly energizing effect student sit-ins and other forms of nonviolent protest had on the quest for equality. Turner holds the Abby Castle Kemper Master Teaching Chair in History at St. Catherine's School in Richmond, Virginia.

SOURCE. Jeffrey A. Turner, "Nonviolent Direct Action and the Rise of a Southern Student Movement," *Sitting In and Speaking Out: Student Movements in the American South 1960–1970*, pp. 43–50. Athens: University of Georgia Press, 2010. Reproduced by permission.

Undergraduates in their late teens or early twenties fueled the sit-in movement, a dramatic, nonviolent challenge to segregation that swept much of the South in the early 1960s, changed the course of the civil rights movement, and laid the groundwork for the 1960s student movement. These activists often saw themselves and were perceived by others through the prism of their age. Theirs was a new generation that would step outside of expectations and challenge authority. . . . But this identity, which emphasized the importance of challenging authority, was intermingled with a separate but related vocational identity. These activists not only were young but also were students, and the fact that their actions grew from a particular educational environment was also significant. The sit-in movement had important implications not only for what became the 1960s generation but also for the South's and the nation's college and university campuses. The introduction of nonviolent direct action opened up new possibilities for student political mobilization on black southern campuses while prompting students to ask new questions about what it meant to be a student and what should constitute a college education.

Nonviolent direct action was not new in 1960. The kinds of actions that fall under its umbrella—boycotts, marches, and an array of physical challenges to segregation that included what would be known by late 1960 as sit-ins—had occurred sporadically since at least the era of Reconstruction. The Fellowship of Reconciliation (FOR) had explored the use of nonviolence to achieve social change since its founding in 1914, and its affiliate, the Congress of Racial Equality (CORE), had been experimenting with forms of nonviolent direct action since its inception in 1942. In 1947, an interracial team of FOR and CORE activists that included Bayard Rustin and James Peck embarked on the Journey of Reconciliation, an interstate bus trip through the Upper South to test a recent Supreme Court ruling ordering the desegregation of interstate bus terminals. During the 1950s, a number of nonviolent challenges to segregated establishments occurred, including lunch-counter demonstrations in Washington, D.C.; St. Louis; Baltimore; and Oklahoma City.

So when four black students from North Carolina Agricultural and Technical College in Greensboro sat down at the city's segregated Woolworth's lunch counter on 1 February 1960, their actions were far from unprecedented. Nevertheless, this episode was different. In contrast to similar demonstrations, this one ignited a movement driven by students and unleashed a host of forces that affected southern politics, culture, and education throughout the decade. The sit-in movement introduced college students as independent political actors capable of altering the region's political landscape and provided a vocabulary and a cache of tactics that drove the movement for years. But the sit-ins also had a tremendous impact on the institutions that housed the foot soldiers of the nonviolent assault on segregation. The sit-in movement drew a national spotlight to the college and university campuses that served as the staging grounds for the student assault on segregation, highlighting these institutions as breeding grounds for idealistic young people seeking to nudge the South toward living up to national ideals of freedom and equality. On individual campuses, the sit-in movement was often a galvanizing event that was at times even celebrated in school yearbooks and alumni publications. But it also at times was a divisive force that set in motion a process that eventually shone a spotlight of a different sort on the South's Negro colleges. The sit-in movement initiated a period of student activism that eventually took aim at the institutions themselves and in the process raised funda-

> "This episode was different. . . . This one ignited a movement."

mental questions about the connections between politics and education as well as the role of segregated colleges in a desegregating South.

Motivations Came from Several Sources

Franklin McCain, one of the four students whose actions initiated the Greensboro movement, later recalled the deep imprint made by the 1957 Little Rock school desegregation crisis. Watching on television, he saw the Arkansas National Guard protecting the black students while angry whites screamed epithets. The scenes planted the seeds of a desire for change. Ezell Blair Jr., another of the Greensboro Four, was influenced by the activism of Mohandas K. Gandhi. "I've never forgotten a television show I saw last year called 'The Pictorial Story

African American students attempt to get served at a lunch counter reserved for white customers in Portsmouth, Virginia, in 1960. (Copyright Bettmann/Corbis/AP Images.)

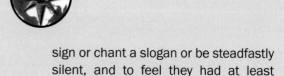

The March Became an Important Form of Protest

As US involvement in the Vietnam War grew, various methods of protest also increased. Some young men burned their draft cards or moved to Canada. Larger numbers of war opponents initiated discussion groups, teach-ins, and petitions. But the biggest protest format was the march.

It seemed somehow fitting; soldiers march, after all. But the antiwar marches, like civil rights marches, were more like informal parades, with crowds of people walking along prominent routes, often concluding with an assembly at a destination of significance.

The march format enabled individuals to be physically part of a mass movement, to be visible or practically anonymous in their protest, to carry a sign or chant a slogan or be steadfastly silent, and to feel they had at least done something positive.

Sizable antiwar marches began in 1965. Early in the year, Students for a Democratic Society (DSD) organized marches to the Oakland Army Terminal, where troops were leaving for Southeast Asia. In April, an SDS-backed antiwar march in Washington, DC, drew about 20,000 people. A huge protest came in April 1967, when about 200,000 marched in New York City. Six months later, approximately 50,000 people surrounded the Pentagon; hundreds were arrested.

More than 2 million people participated in antiwar protests around the country in October 1969, and in the next month 150,000 demonstrated in San Francisco and 500,000 marched in Washington, DC.

of India,'" Blair stated a little more than a month after the demonstrations began. "Gandhi was shown time and time again leaving jail, only to be arrested again." Other students were motivated by a FOR comic book that dramatized the Montgomery Bus Boycott before offering a step-by-step primer from Martin Luther King Jr. in the philosophy and practice of nonviolent direct action. "First, decide what special thing you're going to work on," King said. "In Montgomery, it was buses, somewhere else it might be voting, or schools, or integrated churches. . . .

When you are ready, then go ahead and *don't turn back* no matter how hard the way or how long the struggle."

The numerous forces that generated the sit-in movement had deep roots, but the proximate cause occurred halfway through the 1959–60 academic year. On 1 February 1960, at about 4:45 p.m., four black students from North Carolina Agricultural and Technical College [A&T] entered F. W. Woolworth's, bought some supplies, and sat down for service at the whites-only lunch counter. After being rebuffed by a waitress, they waited for service at the counter until the store closed at 5:30. At that point, concerned about the possibility that they would be prosecuted, the students went to the executive committee of the local chapter of the National Association for the Advancement of Colored People (NAACP) for advice and support. That evening, the four students met with about fifty others from A&T and formed the Student Executive Committee for Justice. The next day, they returned to Woolworth's with twenty-three more students from A&T and four students from Bennett College, a black women's school. All sat at the lunch counter, but no one was served. The demonstrations expanded in the following days, with the group of nonviolent demonstrators growing to include not only other students from A&T and Bennett but also a few white women from the Women's College of the University of North Carolina in Greensboro. . . .

> All sat at the lunch counter, but no one was served.

During the next week, North Carolina students launched additional "sitdown strikes," as they initially were called in the press, in Durham, Winston-Salem, Charlotte, Fayetteville, Raleigh, Elizabeth City, and High Point. In Durham, four white students from Duke University joined black participants at the Woolworth's lunch counter. The demonstration was cut short when the store's manager, C.L. Storm, closed the store at mid-day after receiving a bomb threat. The forty demonstrators moved on to the S.H. Kress and Company store, which also closed soon after their arrival, and then across the street to a Walgreen's drugstore, where they found the lunch counter already roped off and closed. This cat-and-mouse game between student demonstrators and store managers was replicated in other cities. In Greensboro, stores reopened on 8 February only after students agreed to a two-week cooling-off period.

> Skeptics had initially tended to view the sit-ins in light of college students' previous, more frivolous, mass actions.

Sit-down demonstrations spread to Hampton, Virginia, on 11 February and to Rock Hill, South Carolina, the following day. There, demonstrators faced white counterdemonstrators, who shoved the protesters, threw eggs, and tossed a bottle of ammonia. On 13 February, students in Nashville, Tennessee, and Tallahassee, Florida, conducted sit-ins. By this time, not quite two weeks after the initial Greensboro sit-in, observers were beginning to detect the development of something more than a handful of isolated demonstrations against segregation. Skeptics had initially tended to view the sit-ins in light of college students' previous, more frivolous, mass actions—as what journalist Claude Sitton called "another college fad of the 'panty-raid' variety." But, as Sitton noted on 15 February, even skeptics could not summarily dismiss the sit-ins as they spread throughout the region.

By April, seventy-eight cities in thirteen southern states had experienced sit-ins. That month, representatives from college campuses throughout the South gathered in Raleigh, North Carolina, to form an organization, eventually dubbed the Student Nonviolent Coordinating Committee (SNCC) to facilitate communication among the demonstrations. The sit-ins tapered off around the time of spring examinations but picked up again during the summer with the help of high school students. In addition to expanding geographically, the demonstrations also grew in scope. The movement expanded its list of targets to include all types of public accommodations—parks and swimming pools, museums and art galleries.

Imitation of Whites Diminished

The sit-ins initiated a reconsideration or in many cases a discovery of black colleges. College campuses that had been criticized as breeding grounds for apathetic, materialistic students became almost overnight sources for a new militancy that breathed life into the movement for racial equality. "Not long ago the Negro collegian imitated the white collegian," suggested King in a September 1961 article in the *New York Times Magazine*. "In attire, in athletics, in social life, imitation was the rule. For the future, he looked to a professional life as in the image of the middle-class white professional. He imitated with such energy that Gunnar Myrdal described the ambitious Negro as 'an exaggerated American.' Today the imitation has ceased. The Negro collegian now initiates." That same month, a Southern Regional Council study was just as grandiose in its assessment of the impact of the movement: "A solitary instance of spontaneous rebellion has now become a movement of truly massive proportions which has stirred the conscience of the South and of the nation." By then, more than one hundred cities in southern and border states had experienced direct-action demonstrations, with seventy thousand participants and an estimated thirty-six hundred arrests.

On campuses where effective student movements developed, leadership frequently came from nontraditional students. Some had entered college after serving terms in the military or working. Others had previous political experience that gave them insight into mobilizing people. At many schools, student government leaders helped organize demonstrations, thereby hastening mainstream acceptance within the student body. Sympathetic faculty members lent additional support when student movements developed. Finally, the response of an institution's president often played a central role in determining whether a movement died in its infancy or had room to grow. While no college presidents joined the sit-ins, some administrators took a more sympathetic view than did others.

Black Power Evolved as a Movement

Lawrence Muhammad

The following viewpoint discusses William Van Deburg's book, *New Day in Babylon*, which chronicles the black power movement of the 1960s. Lawrence Muhammad, the author of this viewpoint, claims that black power became mainstreamed and many of the officials elected during that era were simply potent but powerless symbols. Van Deburg believes black power was a revolutionary cultural concept. Muhammad is a contributor to the *Nation*, a weekly magazine in the United States.

Readers ready for some serious flashbacks should get William Van Deburg's *New Day in Babylon: The Black Power Movement and American Culture, 1965–1975*. This University of Wisconsin professor of Afro-American studies has collected black power

Stokely Carmichael of the Student Nonviolent Coordinating Committee speaks of black power and the Vietnam War at Florida A&M University in 1968. (AP Images/BH.)

symbolism from novels, stand-up routines, laws, song lyrics, prison time, folk tales, TV shows, cartoons, hair styles, sports competition, ad slogans, street protests, military service, political speeches, religious worship, news reports, college curriculums, and posters.

"Approximately four out of ten Detroit blacks questioned in 1968 approved of dashikis while some 80 percent indicated a liking for soul food and music," Van Deburg quotes a poll. Advertisers promise black female smokers that Eve menthols would "cool a stone fox," he informs. We learn the meaning of "soul," how to "be black" instead of Negro and why in Newark they always asked the time. He even translates the dialect: "If it had been written in black English, the Twenty-third Psalm would have begun: 'The Lord is my main man; I can't dig wanting.'"

Resurrected are largely forgotten events like a walk-out of 500 black workers at a New Jersey auto plant over racial slurs, and the founding of the Republic of New Africa—a bid for black control of some Southern states as reparations for slavery. Van Deburg retells the ex-ploits of personalities as diverse as Nathan Hare, Angela Davis, Sam Greenlee, Andrew Brim-mer, Albert Cleage, Ed Bullins, Hank Ballard, Harry Edwards and Stokely Carmichael.

Throughout the book he upbraids earlier scholars for fixating on politi-cal aspects of the black struggle and ignoring cultural expressions that had lasting impact on the broader white society. But he never really demonstrates how cultural study can clarify this vaguely understood concept called black power. . . .

> "Culturally, though, black power got mainstreamed."

The Mainstreaming of Black Power

Culturally, though, black power got mainstreamed. The thousands of black officials elected during the decade were potent mainly as symbols. Style was the funda-mental distinction between an accommodationist like then-N.A.A.C.P. chief Roy Wilkins and, say, Harry Ed-wards, the big, nappy-headed college professor in shades who made a rights protest with Olympic gold in 1968. Edwards epitomized the new leadership model who didn't soft-pedal his African heritage to succeed. That attitude, emulated in a suddenly contagious surge of ethnic pride, turned into dollar signs as everything from ice cream to Barbie dolls was marketed in black. By the

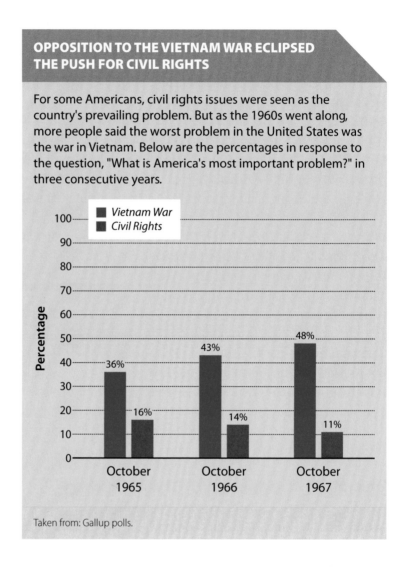

OPPOSITION TO THE VIETNAM WAR ECLIPSED THE PUSH FOR CIVIL RIGHTS

For some Americans, civil rights issues were seen as the country's prevailing problem. But as the 1960s went along, more people said the worst problem in the United States was the war in Vietnam. Below are the percentages in response to the question, "What is America's most important problem?" in three consecutive years.

Taken from: Gallup polls.

1980s, Afrocentric taste was light baggage for *buppies*, those children of a black middle class racially conscious by tradition and long privately convinced that they were better than whites. The black power prerogative, equated to a piece of the pie, remained culturally enshrined despite political retrenchment. George Bush bowed to the 1967 precedent of Thurgood Marshall's appointment to the Supreme Court, albeit with a racial Frankenstein like

PERSPECTIVES ON MODERN WORLD HISTORY

Clarence Thomas. And today we've even got ungrateful recipients of civil rights spoils whining because being black helped them to get where they are. . . .

Black power was a consciousness movement, permeating black society with a progressive new ethic. "Black power was a revolutionary cultural concept," he writes, "a broad, adaptive cultural term serving to connect and illuminate the differing ideological orientations of the movement's supporters." . . .

[Maulana] Karenga, a founder of the Black Arts movement, thought revolutionary fighters first needed ennobling cultural awareness, new values as an antidote to self-taught, self-destructive pathology. The Panthers, who made ghetto desperation a political art, agreed with radical psychiatrist Frantz Fanon that killing the oppressor made you mentally new. . . .

> "The Panthers, who made ghetto desperation a political art, agreed . . . that killing the oppressor made you mentally new."

Van Deburg . . . asserts that the explosion in racial pride made black power historically unique, and not just a continuation of the struggle for equality. "Other modes of comparing these historical apples and oranges, such as tracing the attraction of pan-Africanist sentiment through the centuries, emphasize the predominance of continuity over change," the author writes. "This latter approach suggests that unchanging white attitudes of rejection and ridicule are capable of eliciting essentially the same response from Afro-Americans in different eras. Again, we must ask, 'Why was there a Black Power movement in the late sixties?'" . . .

Van Deburg has produced a comprehensive record of the sixties revolt, a book that evokes the euphoria of rediscovered racial pride. Time will enhance its value as a compact reference for those already in the know, and a useful primer for others who yesterday were referring to "Malcolm Max."

The Students Do Not Understand What They Are Protesting

George F. Kennan

The dissident students of the sixties are not studying the issues they protest, George Kennan declares in the following viewpoint. They are excitedly proclaiming how the world needs to change, but they are avoiding the years of disciplined examination necessary to understand and solve the problems they attack, he contends. And then there are the hippies, who sadly, under the delusion of drugs, believe their insight is growing while in fact the opposite is occurring, Kennan finds. Even so, he says the young people of the sixties are right to blame the older generation for much that is wrong. Kennan's solution: Combine youthful intensity with the best of experience. George F. Kennan (1904–2005) was an influential US diplomat, writer, teacher, and historian.

SOURCE. George F. Kennan, "Rebels Without a Program," *New York Times*, January 21, 1968. Copyright © 2011 by the Seeley G. Mudd Manuscript Library. All rights reserved. Reproduced by permission.

What strikes one first about the angry militancy is the extraordinary degree of certainty by which it is inspired: certainty of one's own rectitude, certainty of the correctness of one's own answers, certainty of the accuracy and profundity of one's own analysis of the problems of contemporary society, certainty as to the iniquity of those who disagree. Of course, vehemence of feeling and a conviction that right is on one's side have seldom been absent from the feelings of politically excited youth. But somehow or other they seem particularly out of place at just this time. Never has there been an era when the problems of public policy even approached in their complexity those by which our society is confronted today, in this age of technical innovation and the explosion of knowledge. The understanding of these problems is something to which one could well give years of disciplined and restrained study, years of the scholar's detachment, years of readiness to reserve judgment while evidence is being accumulated. And this being so, one is struck to see such massive certainties already present in the minds of people who not only *have not* studied very much but presumably *are not* studying a great deal, because it is hard to imagine that the activities to which this aroused portion of our student population gives itself are ones readily compatible with quiet and successful study.

The world seems to be full, today, of embattled students. The public prints are seldom devoid of the record of their activities. Photographs of them may be seen daily: screaming, throwing stones, breaking windows, overturning cars, being beaten or dragged about by police and, in

> That these people are embattled is unquestionable. That they are really students, I must be permitted to doubt.

the case of those on other continents, burning libraries. That these people are embattled is unquestionable. That they are really students, I must be permitted to doubt.

I have heard it freely confessed by members of the revolutionary student generation of Tsarist Russia that, proud as they were of the revolutionary exploits of their youth, they never really learned anything in their university years; they were too busy with politics. The fact of the matter is that the state of being enragé [furious] is simply incompatible with fruitful study. It implies a degree of existing emotional and intellectual commitment which leaves little room for open-minded curiosity.

Students Are Wrong to Blindly Assume They Are Right

I am not saying that students should not be concerned, should not have views, should not question what goes on in the field of national policy and should not voice their questions about it. Some of us, who are older, share many of their misgivings, many of their impulses. Some of us have no less lively a sense of the dangers of the time, and are no happier than they are about a great many things that are now going on. But it lies within the power as well as the duty of all of us to recognize not only the possibility that we might be wrong but the virtual certainty that on some occasions we are bound to be. The fact that this is so does not absolve us from the duty of having views and putting them forward. But it does make it incumbent upon us to recognize the element of doubt that still surrounds the correctness of these views. And if we do that, we will not be able to lose ourselves in transports of moral indignation against those who are of opposite opinion and follow a different line: we will put our views forward only with a prayer for forgiveness for the event that we prove to be mistaken.

I am aware that inhibitions and restraints of this sort on the part of us older people would be attributed by many members of the student left to a sweeping corruption of our moral integrity. Life, they would hold, has impelled us to the making of compromises; and these

compromises have destroyed the usefulness of our contribution. Crippled by our own cowardice, prisoners of the seamy adjustments we have made in order to be successfully a part of the American establishment, we are regarded as no longer capable of looking steadily into the strong clear light of truth. . . .

The Hippies Are Self-Deluded

So much, then, for the angry ones. Now, a word about the others: the quiescent ones, the hippies and the flower people.

In one sense, my feeling for these people is one of pity, not unmixed, in some instances, with horror. I am sure that they want none of this pity. They would feel that it comes to them for the wrong reasons. If they feel sorry for themselves, it is because they see themselves as the victims

Some consider events like this Honor America Day Smoke-In—held by marijuana activists at the Mall in Washington, DC, in 1970—an example of the student movement's misguided efforts. (David Fenton/ Getty Images.)

of a harsh, hypocritical and unworthy adult society. If I feel sorry for them, it is because I see them as the victims of certain great and destructive philosophic errors.

One of these errors—and it is one that affects particularly those who take drugs, but not those alone—is the belief that the human being has marvelous resources within himself that can be released and made available to him merely by the passive submission to certain sorts of stimuli: by letting esthetic impressions of one sort or another roll over him or by letting his psychic equilibrium be disoriented by chemical agencies that give him the sensation of experiencing tremendous things. Well, it is true that human beings sometimes have marvelous resources within themselves. It is also true that these resources are capable, ideally, of being released and made available to the man that harbors them and through him to others, and sometimes are so released. But it is not true that they can be released by hippie means.

> It is only through effort, through doing, through action . . . that man grows creatively.

It is only through effort, through doing, through action—never through passive experience—that man grows creatively. It is only by volition and effort that he becomes fully aware of what he has in him of creativity and becomes capable of embodying it, of making it a part of himself, of communicating it to others. There is no pose more fraudulent—and students would do well to remember this when they look at each other—than that of the individual who pretends to have been exalted and rendered more impressive by his communion with some sort of inner voice whose revelations he is unable to describe or to enact. And particularly is this pose fraudulent when the means he has chosen to render himself susceptible to this alleged revelation is the deliberate disorientation of his own psychic system; for it may be said with surety that any artificial intervention of this sort—

into the infinitely delicate balance that nature created in the form of man's psychic make-up—produces its own revenge, takes its own toll, proceeds at the cost of the true creative faculties and weakens rather than strengthens.

The second error I see in the outlook of these people is the belief in the possibility and validity of a total personal permissiveness. They are misjudging, here, the innermost nature of man's estate. There is not, and cannot be, such a thing as total freedom. The normal needs and frail-ties of the body, not to mention the elementary demands of the soul itself, would rule that out if nothing else did. But beyond that, any freedom from something implies a freedom to something. And because our reality is a com-plex one, in which conflicts of values are never absent, there can be no advance toward any particular objective, not even the pursuit of pleasure, that does not imply the sacrifice of other possible objectives. Freedom, for this reason, is definable only in terms of the obligations and restraints and sacrifices it accepts. It exists, as a concept, only in relationship to something else which is by defi-nition its opposite: and that means commitment, duty, self-restraint.

> "There is not, and cannot be, such a thing as total freedom."

Every great artist has known this. Every great phi-losopher has recognized it. It has lain at the basis of Judaic-Christian teaching. Tell me what framework of discipline you are prepared to accept, and I will attempt to tell you what freedom might mean for you. But if you tell me that you are prepared to accept no framework of discipline at all, then I will tell you, as [Russia writer Fy-odor] Dostoyevsky told his readers, that you are destined to become the most unfree of men; for freedom begins only with the humble acceptance of membership in, and subordination to, a natural order of things, and it grows only with struggle, and self-discipline, and faith. . . .

The Older Generation Is Much to Blame

Now, being myself a father, I am only too well aware that people of my generation cannot absolve ourselves of a heavy responsibility for the state of mind in which these young people find themselves. We are obliged to recognize here, in the myopia and the crudities of *their* extremism, the reflection of our own failings: our smugness, our timidity, our faint-heartedness and in some instances our weariness, our apathy in the face of great and obvious evils.

I am also aware that, while their methods may not be the right ones, and while their discontent may suffer in its effectiveness from the concentration on negative goals, the degree of their concern over the present state of our country and the dangers implicit in certain of its involvements is by no means exaggerated. This is a time in our national life more serious, more menacing, more crucial, than any I have ever experienced or ever hoped to experience. Not since the civil conflict of a century ago has this country, as I see it, been in such great danger; and the most excruciating aspect of this tragic state of affairs is that so much of this danger comes so largely from within, where we are giving it relatively little official attention, and so little of it comes, relatively speaking, from the swamps and jungles of Southeast Asia into which we are pouring our treasure of young blood and physical resources.

> Not since the civil conflict of a century ago has this country, as I see it, been in such great danger.

For these reasons, I do not mean to make light of the intensity of feeling by which this student left is seized. Nor do I mean to imply that people like myself can view this discontent from some sort of smug Olympian detachment, as though it were not our responsibility, as though it were not in part our own ugly and decadent face that we see in this distorted mirror. None of us could have any justification for attempting to enter into communication with these people if we did not recognize, along with the justification for their unhappiness, our own responsibility in the creation of it, and if we did not accompany our appeal to them with a profession of readiness to join them, where they want us to, in the attempt to find better answers to many of these problems.

I am well aware that in approaching them in this way and in taking issue as I have with elements of their outlook and their behavior, it is primarily myself that I have committed, not them. I know that behind all the extremisms—all the philosophical errors, all the egocentricities and all the oddities of dress and deportment—we have to do here with troubled and often pathetically appealing people, acting, however wisely or unwisely, out of sincerity and idealism, out of the unwillingness to accept a meaningless life and a purposeless society.

Well, this is not the life, and not the sort of society, that many of us would like to leave behind us in this country when our work is done. How wonderful it would be, I sometimes think to myself, if we and they—experience on the one hand, strength and enthusiasm on the other—could join forces.

The New Left Embraced Progressive Goals Yet Excluded Gays and Women

Ian Lekus

In the early 1960s, some groups of students put forth views on issues that were strongly liberal yet distinctly different from positions traditionally taken by the political left in the United States, notes historian Ian Lekus in the following viewpoint. For what became known as the New Left, essential issues included race, class, sexual freedom, poverty, the Vietnam War, and university and government repression. The concept of authentic living was prized, Lekus writes. Yet inconsistencies surfaced, he finds, particularly regarding heterosexual males' behavior toward women, lesbians, gay men, and bisexual people. Lekus, a lecturer in history at Harvard University, studies, writes about, and teaches courses in gender issues.

SOURCE. Ian Lekus, "New Left and Student Movements," *Encyclopedia of Lesbian, Gay, Bisexual and Transgendered History in America,* vol. 1E, Marc Stein, ed., pp. 325–329. Detroit: Charles Scribner's Sons, 2003. © 2003 Cengage Learning. Reproduced by permission.

In June 1962 several dozen white student activists from East Coast and Midwestern colleges gathered in Michigan to discuss their shared concerns about racism, poverty, the nuclear arms race, and the prevailing Cold War culture of complacency. These students, gathering under the aegis of Students for a Democratic Society (SDS), issued the Port Huron Statement, in which they outlined their vision for rejuvenating U.S. politics and society through participatory democracy. Focusing on the intertwined problems of racial and economic injustice, SDS members sought to organize a white student movement parallel to the civil rights struggle. They also positioned SDS to serve as the nexus of this New Left in a role comparable to that claimed by the Student Nonviolent Coordinating Committee (SNCC), organized in 1960 by students from historically black colleges in the Jim Crow South.

The New Left of the 1960s staked out a politics of anti-anticommunism, distinguishing it from the Old Left of the interwar and Cold War decades. Whereas Old Leftists drew upon Marxist-Leninist analyses and models of organizing, New Leftists refused to be drawn into the Cold War communist-anticommunist dichotomy. Instead, they argued that anticommunism distracted citizens from the genuine ills of U.S. society and condemned the reigning corporate liberalism that served the interests of the wealthy rather than the economically disadvantaged.

Along with the questions of race and class that dominated early New Left community projects, student activists addressed local concerns, as when the Free Speech Movement organized in Berkeley in response to attempts by University of California officials to regulate political activity on campus property. As the decade wore on, however, the escalating Vietnam War took precedence for the New Left. Draft resisters organized across the nation, using the famed slogans "Hell No, We Won't Go!"

Establishment of Rights Was a Milestone of the Decade

In the United States, gains in civil rights—including the legal rights of women—appear to be the most clear-cut achievement of the 1960s activist movements.

Certainly the feminist movement did a great deal to raise awareness of unfairness, the antiwar movement led a president away from seeking reelection, and the rising prominence of youth in general altered US culture significantly. Yet it was in civil rights that the laws changed then in major ways, because activists—largely students—risked their futures and even their lives for the cause.

From sit-ins in North Carolina to youth marches in Alabama to college journalists who founded and operated the *Southern Courier*—a newspaper that during its three years revealed widespread racial injustice—students brought energy, intellect, and idealism to the effort that resulted in the Civil Rights Act of 1964 and the Voting Rights Act of 1965. A century after the Civil War ostensibly ended slavery, no longer could any citizen's rights be limited on the basis of race, color, gender, religion, or national origin.

and "Girls Say Yes to Guys Who Say No" (to the draft, that is). Increasingly, movement leaders shifted from condemning the "evils in America" to the "evils of America," SDS historian Kirkpatrick Sale has noted, and began advocating violent means to social change. New Leftists cheered on North Vietnamese leader Ho Chi Minh and the National Liberation Front of South Vietnam. White students led major rebellions at Columbia University and many other campuses, while rifle-toting black power activists took over the student union at Cornell University in 1969. As anger about the war and other policies of the [Lyndon] Johnson and [Richard] Nixon presidential administrations brought hundreds of thousands of students into the movement, the New Left became increasingly decentralized. SDS eventually disintegrated as a series of Marxist-Leninist factions battled to take control over the organization's national leadership. Nonetheless, New Left organizers continued to address the Vietnam War, racism, and newer concerns such as feminism, the ecology, and gay liberation through the early 1970s.

Gains Were Uneven

Throughout the 1960s, lesbians, gay men, and bisexuals played critical roles in local and national student movement politics. . . . The gay liberation movement's sweeping vision of democratic social transformation and ardent espousal of "coming out" derived directly from its members' experiences in the New Left and from attempting to live out what movement historian Doug Rossinow described as "the politics of authenticity." However, the student movement often offered an uncomfortable home to those men and women for whom authentic living included acting upon one's sexual attraction to the same or both sexes.

> Student activists of all sexualities shared similar goals.

Student activists of all sexualities shared similar goals: ending poverty and racism; organizing disenfranchised Americans to assert the power to improve the material conditions of their lives; stopping the Vietnam War; and curbing the excesses of the military-industrial complex. But despite the self-proclaimed radicalism of many heterosexual men in the New Left, they frequently shared the antigay attitudes of the Cold War society in which they grew up. Generally dominating New Left organizations, these men often gay-baited their opponents and cajoled male recruits into

Demonstrations for gay rights, like this one in Philadelphia on July 4, 1967, were not generally included in the student movements of the 1960s. (AP Images.)

proving their masculinity. They frequently organized women in and out of the movement based on whom they were dating at a given moment, effectively dividing New Left women into girlfriends who mimeographed and made coffee on the one hand and desexualized leaders who were essentially accepted as "one of the boys" on the other. Frequently, these men justified their own antigay and antifeminist rhetoric and practices by identifying as authentic revolutionary attitudes the homophobia and misogyny that they perceived as inherent to white working-class, black power, and Third World movements and cultures. Antigay movement cultures were further exacerbated by infiltrators from the Federal Bureau of Investigation and other state and local government authorities, whose agents spread rumors about the sexual orientation of specific activists in order to discredit them. Gay-baiting took its toll upon unknown numbers of lesbians, gay men, and bisexuals, compelling some to lie and hide their sexual orientation while driving others from the movement altogether. . . .

While most New Leftists brought to the movement the antigay attitudes instilled in them as children of the Cold War 1950s, the trust and candor earned during the ongoing work of discussing, planning, and carrying out social change provided some heterosexual activists with the experiential knowledge necessary to challenge these homophobic assumptions.

Young Women Defined Their Own Liberation Movement

Kathie Sarachild

For women to achieve equality with men, they had to address root problems in society, Kathie Sarachild asserts in the following viewpoint. First, women had to raise their own consciousness without men present, to become fully aware of how they had gone along with inequality, she says. They had to give less priority to simply being attractive. Women had to study and apply their own experience to determine how to change society, and the civil rights movement provided strong examples for action. Women had to be willing to endure sharp criticism, but the rewards of a liberation movement were exciting and important, Sarachild concludes. Kathie Sarachild was a founding member of New York Radical Women (1967) and Redstockings of the Women's Liberation Movement (1969). She is currently the director of the Redstockings Archives for Action.

SOURCE. Kathie Sarachild, "Consciousness-Raising: A Radical Weapon," comments to the First National Conference of Stewardesses for Women's Rights, March 12, 1973. Reproduced by permission.

To understand what feminist consciousness-raising is all about, it is important to remember that it began as a program among women who all considered themselves radicals.

Before we go any further, let's examine the word "radical." It is a word that is often used to suggest extremist, but actually it doesn't mean that. The dictionary says radical means root, coming from the Latin word for root. And that is what we meant by calling ourselves radicals. We were interested in getting to the roots of problems in society. You might say we wanted to pull up weeds in the garden by their roots, not just pick off the leaves at the top to make things look good momentarily. Women's Liberation was started by women who considered themselves radicals in this sense.

Our aim in forming a women's liberation group was to start a *mass movement of women* to put an end to the barriers of segregation and discrimination based on sex. We knew radical thinking and radical action would be necessary to do this. We also believed it necessary to form Women's Liberation groups which excluded men from their meetings.

Examining the Oppression of Women

In order to have a radical approach, to get to the root, it seemed logical that we had to study the situation of women, not just take random action. How best to do this came up in the women's liberation group I was in—New York Radical Women, one of the first in the country—shortly after the group had formed. We were planning our first public action and wandered into a discussion about what to do next. One woman in the group, Ann Forer, spoke up: "I think we have a lot more to do just in the area of raising our consciousness," she said. "Raising consciousness?" I wondered what she meant by that. I'd never heard it applied to women before.

"I've only begun thinking about women as an oppressed group," she continued, "and each day, I'm still learning more about it—my consciousness gets higher."

Now I didn't consider that I had just started thinking about the oppression of women. In fact, I thought of myself as having done lots of thinking about it for quite a while, and lots of reading too. But then Ann went on to give an example of something she'd noticed that turned out to be a deeper way of seeing it for me, too.

> I just sat there listening to her describe all the false ways women have to act.

"I think a lot about being attractive," Ann said. "People don't find the real self of a woman attractive."

And then she went on to give some examples. And I just sat there listening to her describe all the false ways women have to act: playing dumb, always being agreeable, always being nice, not to mention what we had to do to our bodies, with the clothes and shoes we wore, the diets we had to go through, going blind not wearing glasses, all because men didn't find our real selves, our human freedom, our basic humanity "attractive." And I realized I still could learn a lot about how to understand and describe the particular oppression of women in ways that could reach other women in the way this had just reached me. The whole group was moved as I was, and we decided on the spot that what we needed—in the words Ann used—was to "raise our consciousness some more."

Focusing on the Present Reality

At the next meeting there was an argument in the group about how to do this. One woman—Peggy Dobbins—said that what she wanted to do was make a very intensive study of all the literature on the question of whether there really were any biological differences between men and women. I found myself angered by that idea.

"I think it would be a waste of time," I said. "For every scientific study we quote, the opposition can find their scientific studies to quote. Besides, the question is what we want to be, what we think we are, not what some authorities in the name of science are arguing over what we are. It is scientifically impossible to tell what the biological differences are between men and women—if there are any besides the obvious physical ones—until all the social and political factors applying to men and women are equal. Everything we have to know, have to prove, we can get from the realities of our own lives. For instance, on the subject of women's intelligence. We know from our own experience that women play dumb for men because, if we're too smart, men won't like us. I know, because I've done it. We've all done it. Therefore, we can simply deduce that women are smarter than men are aware of, and that there are a lot of women around

Women protest against the Miss America Pageant on the boardwalk in Atlantic City, New Jersey, in September 1969. (Santi Visalli Inc./ Getty Images.)

who are a lot smarter than they look and smarter than anybody but themsleves and maybe a few of their friends know."

In the end the group decided to raise its consciousness by studying women's lives by topics like childhood, jobs, motherhood, etc. We'd do any outside reading we wanted to and thought was important. But our starting point for discussion, as well as our test of the accuracy of what any of the books said, would be the actual experience we had in these areas. One of the questions, suggested by Ann Forer, we would bring at all times to our studies would be—who and what has an interest in maintaining the oppression in our lives. The kind of actions the groups should engage in, at this point, we decided—acting upon an idea of Carol Hanisch, another woman in the group—would be consciousness-raising actions . . . actions brought to the public for the specific purpose of challenging old ideas and raising new ones, the very same issues of feminism we were studying ourselves. Our role was not to be a "service organization," we decided, nor a large "membership organization." What we were talking about being was, in effect, Carol explained, a "zap" action, political agitation and education group something like what the Student Non-Violent Coordinating Committee (S.N.C.C.) had been. We would be the first to dare to say and do the undareable, what women really felt and wanted. The first job now was to raise awareness and understanding, our own and others—awareness that would prompt people to organize and to act on a mass scale.

> We would be the first to dare to say and do the undareable.

The decision to emphasize our own feelings and experiences as women and to test all generalizations and reading we did by our own experience was actually the scientific method of research. We were in effect repeating the 17th century challenge to science to scholasticism:

"study nature, not books," and put all theories to the test of living practice and action. It was also a method of radical organizing tested by other revolutions. We were applying to women and to ourselves as women's liberation organizers the practice a number of us had learned as organizers in the civil rights movement in the South in the early 1960's.

Consciousness-raising—studying the whole gamut of women's lives, starting with the full reality of one's own—would also be a way of keeping the movement radical by preventing it from getting sidetracked into single issue reforms and single issue organizing. It would be a way of carrying theory about women further than it had ever been carried before, as the groundwork for achieving a radical solution for women as yet attained nowhere.

> We felt that all women would have to see the fight of women as their own.

It seemed clear that knowing how our own lives related to the general condition of women would make us better fighters on behalf of women as a whole. We felt that all women would have to see the fight of women as their own, not as something just to help "other women," that they would have to see this truth about their own lives before they would fight in a radical way for anyone. "Go fight your own oppressors," [SNCC leader] Stokely Carmichael had said to the white civil rights workers when the black power movement began. "You don't get radicalized fighting other people's battles," as Beverly Jones put it in the pioneering essay "Toward a Female Liberation Movement."

The Opposition Was Astounding

There turned out to be tremendous resistance to women's simply studying their situation, especially without men in the room. In the beginning we had set out to do our studying in order to take better action. We hadn't

MORE WOMEN WORK, BUT MEN CONTINUE TO MAKE MORE MONEY

Effective in 1964, the Equal Pay Act made it illegal to pay women less than men for the same job. However, women continued to work in lower-paying jobs.

Number of Men and Women in US Workforce

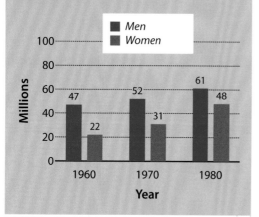

Women's Earnings as a Percentage of Men's

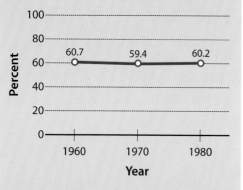

Note: In 2010, women earned 81% of what men earned.

Taken from: US Census Bureau and the National Committee on Pay Equity.

realized that just studying this subject and naming the problem and problems would be a radical action in itself, action so radical as to engender tremendous and persistent opposition from directions that still manage to flabbergast me. The opposition often took the form of misinterpretations and misrepresentations of what we were doing that no amount of explanation on our part seemed able to set straight. The methods and assumptions behind consciousness-raising essentially grew out of both the scientific and radical political traditions, but when we applied them to women's situation, a whole lot of otherwise "scientific" and "radical" people—especially men—just couldn't see this.

Whole areas of women's lives were declared off limits to discussion. The topics we were talking about in our groups were dismissed as "petty" or "not political." Often these were the key areas in terms of how women are oppressed as a particular group—like housework, childcare and sex. Everybody from Republicans to Communists said that they agreed that equal pay for equal work was a valid issue and deserved support. But when women wanted to try to figure out why we weren't *getting* equal pay for equal work anywhere, and wanted to take a look in these areas, then what we were doing wasn't politics, economic or even study at all, but "therapy," something that women had to work out for themselves individually.

When we began analyzing these problems in terms of male chauvinism, we were suddenly the living proof of how backward women are. Although we had taken radical political action and risks many times before, and would act again and again, when we discussed male chauvinism, suddenly we were just women who complained all the time, who stayed in the personal realm and never took any action.

Some people said outright they thought what we were doing was dangerous. When we merely brought up concrete examples in our lives of discrimination against women, or exploitation of women, we were accused of "man-hating" or "sour grapes." These were more efforts to keep the issues and ideas we were discussing out of the realm of subjects of genuine study and debate by defining them as psychological delusions.

"Some people said outright they thought what we were doing was dangerous.

And when we attempted to describe the realities of our lives in certain ways, however logical—for instance, when we said that men oppressed women, or that all men were among the beneficiaries in the oppression of women—some people really got upset. "You can't say that men are the oppressors of women! Men are oppressed, too! And women discriminate against women!" Now it would seem to go without saying that if women have a secondary status in the society compared to men, and are treated as secondary creatures, then the beneficiaries would be those with the primary status.

Our meetings were called coffee klatches, hen parties or bitch sessions. We responded by saying, "Yes, bitch, sisters, bitch," and by calling coffee klatches a historic form of women's resistance to oppression. The name calling and attacks were for us a constant source of irritation and sometimes of amazement as they often came from other radicals who we thought would welcome this new mass movement of an oppressed group. Worse yet, the lies prevented some women we would have liked to reach from learning about what we were really doing.

The Miss America Contest Brought Widespread Attention

There was no denying, though, that we ourselves were learning a tremendous amount from the discussions and were finding them very exciting. From our consciousness-raising meetings was coming the writing which was formulating basic theory for the women's liberation movement. Shulamith Firestone, who wrote the book *The Dialectic of Sex*, Anne Koedt, who wrote the essay "The Myth of the Vaginal Orgasm," Pat Mainardi, who wrote the essay "The Politics of Housework," Carol Hanisch, who wrote the essay "The Personal Is Political," Kate Millett, who wrote *Sexual Politics*, Cindy Cisler, who led the ground-breaking abortion law repeal fight in New York, Rosalyn Baxandall, Irene Peslikis, Ellen Willis, Robin Morgan and many others participated in these discussions. Most of us had thought we were only beginning to have a radical understanding of women—and of other issues of class, race and revolutionary change.

Our group was growing rapidly. Other women were as fascinated as we about the idea of doing something politically about aspects of our lives as women that we never thought could be dealt with politically, that we thought we would just have to work out as best we could alone. Most of these issues the National Organization for Women (NOW) wouldn't touch. Was it because these subjects were "petty" or really hitting at the heart of things—areas of deepest humiliation for all women? Neither was NOW then organizing consciousness-raising groups. This only happened after 1968, when the new and more radical groups formed, with a mass perspective. Our group's first public action after putting out a journal was an attempt to reach the masses with our ideas on one of those so-called petty topics: the issue of appearance. We protested and picketed the Miss America Contest, throwing high heels, girdles and other objects of female torture into a freedom trash can. It was this action in 1968 which first awakened widespread awareness of the new "Women's Liberation Movement," capturing world interest and giving the movement its very name.

The Counterculture, 1964–1965

Tom Hayden

Within just a few years, the prevailing spirit of the youth movement shifted from the constructive possibilities of reform to a split
between outright resistance and escapist drug use, Tom Hayden
argues in the following viewpoint. This shift was fueled by the rigidity of the older mainstream culture, he says, and the splintering of
young people came to mean that the student movement's original
goals would be largely thwarted. The counterculture became a
useful target for conservatives, who then made gains politically,
he finds. Hayden concludes that the resulting government stalled
racial progress, blocked diversity, and pursued the catastrophi-
cally destructive Vietnam War. Tom Hayden was a founder of the
Students for a Democratic Society and principal writer of its Port
Huron statement. He has written seventeen books. Beginning in
1983 he served for eighteen years in the California legislature.

SOURCE. Tom Hayden, "The Counterculture, 1964–1965," *The
Long Sixties: From 1960 to Barack Obama,* pp. 43–47. Boulder,
Colorado: Paradigm Publishers, 2009. Copyright © 2009 by Paradigm
Publishers. All rights reserved. Reproduced by permission.

The possibilities of reform grew dimmer, the meaning of life more absurd. Those in power, with the acquiescence of an older generation, began to rebuff, dismiss, and alienate the new generation. For us, a generational lifespan could be defined as the difference between 1963's hopeful "Blowing in the Wind" and 1968's "Sympathy for the Devil." In SDS only five years separated the Port Huron generation from the resistance generation. The shift from SNCC to the Black Panther Party, the Brown Berets, the Young Lords, and the Third World Liberation Front at San Francisco State all spanned the same brief period of time.

It is no accident that the so-called counterculture began mushrooming as the space for political opportunities shriveled, appearing to be a mirage. If our elders were clueless, not listening, did not know what was happening, what was the point of meeting them halfway with reasonable demands they would inevitably reject? The distancing became somatic, a revulsion felt in our bodies. Young men's hair grew longer overnight. Bras fell off. The clothing one wore became a badge of separation. Widening the generation gap was the arrival of a drug culture, turning a majority of young people into criminal outlaws in the eyes of the authorities. Marijuana use seemed universal. Then came acid, spiraling out of CIA laboratories and promoted by renowed artists and intellectuals. Along came the other psychedelics: peyote, mescaline, and mushrooms. Presumably by accident, LSD exploded on the streets in early 1965, just as the Vietnam escalation unfolded.

I am not arguing that the CIA dosed the younger generation as a counter-insurgency tool, but there is substantial evidence that LSD was developed and used in CIA covert operations and mind-control programs like MK-ULTRA and that places such as Haight-Ashbury were monitored by the CIA as if it were experimenting with human guinea pigs. It was estimated that 4 million

Americans were trying acid by 1965, on average once every three or four months. Counter-culture ghettos arose from the Haight to the East Village. Perhaps bohemias are inevitable under any circumstances, and great art is always oppositional, but there was a definite link between the closed rigidity of the dominant culture and the forming of the counterculture. Cultural revolution overtook, competed with, and, it could be argued, weakened the idea of radical political reform.

The counterculture fit the model of movements erupting from the margins to become mainstream a few years later. *Hair* was on Broadway by 1967, the same year that "All You Need Is Love" was reaching a satellite audience of 700 million. Soon professors were predicting the "greening" of all America. Buddhism crossed the ocean. A new spirituality insisted that psychedelics were the gateway to transcendence of the ego. The revolution, some thought, would be blissful evolution, flower children wielding flower power. These feelings were widespread, whether a person was dropping out in the Haight, gardening naked on a commune, escaping the draft by fleeing to Canada, or marching on the Pentagon. The commingling was reflected in the defendants in the Chicago conspiracy trial, where the government chose to prosecute the New Left, the Yippies (Youth International Party), and the Black Panthers all at once and where the defense introduced into evidence an "om" from Allen Ginsberg. Among the high points were the Human Be-In in Golden Gate Park (1966); the Monterey Pop Festival, which replaced progressive folk music with acid rock (1967); and the three-day Woodstock Festival (August 15–18, 1969), where three hundred thousand young people celebrated the rude birth of a new nation. To many, it seemed that the Woodstock Nation would overcome.

> The revolution, some thought, would be blissful evolution.

The Student Strikes of 1970

The 1960s ended, but the Vietnam War went on, to the increasing frustration of many Americans, including students. Responding to President Richard Nixon's expansion of the war into Cambodia and the National Guard's killing of four students at Kent State University in Ohio, students across the country held strikes during May 1970.

On some campuses, students occupied administration and classroom buildings and shut down classes for days at a time. Protest marchers denounced the president and the draft. Dozens of firebombings were reported.

More than a few faculty members joined the effort. Although the strike was a national event, what happened from campus to campus was generally up to individual student leaders—as well as the reactions of individual authorities.

By some tallies, about 4 million students struck at 450 universities, colleges, and high schools. The vast extent of the student protest had an impact on even the president and his top leaders, according to one of them, Henry Kissinger, who wrote later in *The White House Years*: "The very fabric of government was falling apart. The executive branch was shell-shocked. After all, their children and their friends' children took part in the demonstrations."

This was an acid dream. The counterculture was most robust among a vast cross section of young white people who were isolated from the black, Chicano, and Native American communities they revered at a distance. Although hating Vietnam and joining the occasional mass march, the counterculture was inherently uninterested in door-to-door community organizing or electoral campaigns. This was also a generational fight, pitting the young against their parents. To the extent that it could be said to be revolutionary, the counterculture was in the great tradition of antibourgeois artists and bohemians who defined themselves by flaunting mainstream ways. Its very nature fueled the backlash among "clueless" Americans who could be recruited to calls for law and order. Although the passing of years gave the counterculture more acceptance, even co-optation into consumer culture, the critical period between 1965 and 1972 was one of conservative advantage, with lasting political consequences.

At the height of the counterculture concerts, be-ins, and festivals, a later declassified CIA report optimistically viewed the mass spectacles as "a new political force that would be an alternative to street action for young people." In retrospect, the counterculture definitely depoliticized the movement while escalating the backlash. The new drugs were reminiscent of the distribution of alcohol for Americans Indians, gin for the "gin mills" of Irish and British workers, and Britain's introduction of opium into China. Tolerance of cultural "revolutions" and various forms of spiritual escapism was an old imperial tactic employed to siphon energy away from threatening political movements. The counterculture could be channeled either into counterproductive purposes or into a limited revolution of style, a youth market rather than a youth nation. Although Timothy Leary, encouraged by Marshall McLuhan to advertise "a new and improved accelerated brain," was advising millions of young people to merely turn on, tune in, and drop out, police were cracking down on and infiltrating longhairs everywhere, and politicians such as Ronald Reagan and Richard Nixon, advised by J. Edgar Hoover, were exploiting white

> Politicians . . . were exploiting white middle-class anxieties.

middle-class anxieties to win offices from Sacramento to the White House. It was a strategy for a conservative political realignment as drafted by Kevin Phillips, senior adviser to Nixon beginning in 1967.

Whereas the reactionary countermovement had been confined to the racist South in the first years of the sixties, now the backlash came from parents and working-class people in the Democratic suburbs coast to coast. To many in the counterculture, however, the backlash did not matter very much at all, in fact was an outcome that might be desired if the point was to be a prankster, to freak out "straight" society. So Ken Kesey's brilliant 1962 novel *One Flew over the Cuckoo's Nest*, like J.D. Salinger's *Catcher in the Rye*, Paul Goodman's *Growing Up Absurd,* and R.D. Laing's radical critique of psychiatry, virtually turned psychosis into a revolutionary stance, the only rational response to an insane society. Where Rosa Parks had ridden a bus to defy segregation, Kesey, Neal Cassady, and friends painted a bus in psychedelic colors, dubbed it "Furthur," and drove it across America as a "happening." Next came Kool-Aid Acid Tests in public parks, acid-driven celebrations of psychedelic consciousness, and constant "pranking" of mainstream consciousness.

> Instead of patience, the young flew on acid, then on speed.

Because the elders had failed us, it seemed, all that was left was for us to fail them. Since politics and persuasion were hopeless, it was time to break on through "the doors of perception" to the other side. Instead of patience, the young flew on acid, then on speed. . . . The toil of artists dead from overdoses included Brian Epstein (1967), Frankie Lymon (1968), Brian Jones (1969), Janis Joplin (1970), Jimi Hendrix (1970), Alan "Blind Owl" Wilson (1970), Jim Morrison (1971), Billy Murcia (1972), Danny Whitten (1972), Gram Parsons (1973), Nick Drake (1974), Tim Buckley (1975), Phil

Ochs (1976), and Keith Moon (1978). My friend and co-conspirator Abbie Hoffman overdosed and died on April 12, 1989. My friend and co-conspirator Rennie Davis, the greatest organizer I ever knew, went to India in 1972 at the height of the Vietnam War and came back transformed into a devout follower of a fourteen-year-old boy-god. As my friend Gary Snyder told me years later, the mixture of dings with Western individualism and materialism was a destructive brew.

Things would become worse. On August 9, 1969, the Charles Manson commune, with roots in both the Haight and the Southern California dropout scene, massacred the pregnant actress Sharon Tate and four others in her Hollywood Hills home. . . . Then on December 6, 1969, the Hells Angels, long courted by many in the counterculture, beat to death a black man, Meredith Hunter, in full view of the Rolling Stones and their fans at an Altamont concert. "If you were forced to select an event that 'ended' the optimistic promise of the Haight-Ashbury era, Altamont would be as good as any," wrote Digger communard Peter Coyote in his autobiography.

I cannot be completely judgmental about those crazy years, however. There was nothing wrong with smoking marijuana in a society of tobacco smokers and alcoholics. There was nothing wrong with sex out of marriage or monogamy, or communal living, or gay/lesbian sex for consenting partners. There was nothing wrong with obscenity. There was nothing wrong with hitchhiking or dropping out, and who in their right mind could complain about heretical poetry? The extremes of destruction do not render the behavior illegitimate. The counterculture was ahead of its time, an extreme response to extremes of conformity. The response to it was a systemic overreaction, sometimes spontaneous and understandable but too often deliberate and political. . . . The entire youth revolt was in response to a failure of the elders. It was the elders, after all, who insisted on the

Photo on previous page: Activists protest the detention of their leader, Tom Hayden, during ongoing demonstrations at the 1968 Democratic National Convention in Chicago. (Art Shay/Time & Life Pictures/Getty Images.)

straitjacket conformity, the delay and denial of blatant inequalities, the suffocating repression and waning of hope that drove so many of their own children into an alienated search for new identities. The elders' promotion of extreme self-interested individualism, extolled in the novels of Ayn Rand, prompted an opposing quest to drop out and destroy the ego altogether, to be gratefully dead instead of gratefully pacified.

Young People Turned from Radical Politics to Mystical Religions

Stephen A. Kent

As the sixties ended, many young people delved into alternative religions, Stephen Kent notes in the following viewpoint. They were driven chiefly by frustration over the youth movement's failure to end the Vietnam War, he concludes. Their heightened idealism had been crushed by events ranging from the assassination of President John F. Kennedy to the persistence of the war and its draft calls, Kent writes. With political participation appearing futile as well as spiritually costly, he says, mystic religions became the resulting escape route. An author of numerous journal articles, Stephen A. Kent was a professor in the sociology department of the University of Alberta, Canada.

SOURCE. Stephen A. Kent, "Introduction," *From Slogans to Mantras: Social Protest and Religious Conversion in the Late Vietnam Era.* Syracuse, NY: Syracuse University Press, 2001, pp. 1–5. Copyright © 2001 by Syracuse University Press. All rights reserved. Reproduced by permission.

As the era of political protests faded in the early 1970s, the United States and other Western countries experienced dramatic numbers of youth converting to new and exotic religions. Where the late 1960s had been characterized by explosions of youthful protest over social issues, in the new decade many of those who had been protesting were turning instead to new religions or undertaking unorthodox spiritual disciplines. Gurus, swamis, teachers, spiritual masters, and "enlightened souls" attracted tens of thousands of baby boomers into what often were unusual and controversial practices.

During this period, American social commentators—including political and social activists observing the actions of their comrades—noticed that a major cultural shift was occurring. Dozens of alternative newspapers carried articles about this emerging cultural pattern, although no uniformity existed either in their portrayal of unfolding events or in their evaluation of them. Some articles spoke highly of the new social values that religion would bring into discussions about political and social change; others reviled former activists who seemingly were turning away from direct social critique and confrontation. Likewise, many social commentators pondered the impact that these unorthodox religious expressions would have on individuals, their generation, and the diminishing political protest movement. In the early 1970s, these topics were among the burning questions of the day. . . .

I contend that young adults' attraction to an array of religious figures and practices in the late Vietnam War period was a direct response to their negative experiences with social—especially political—protest. When thousands of youth went from chanting political slogans to chanting meditational mantras or prayers, this transition reflected the social and political frustrations and disappointments of a generation in despair. Certainly, the shift from radical politics to mystical religion was not the only direction that youth took as the 1960s wound down and fragmented. The women's movement, ecology, rural living, communes, gay rights, and other social movements also captured the attention of young adults who had been touched by a shared dream of love and peace. The emerging religious phenomenon, however, was the most dramatic and among the most controversial of youth culture options, and it has proven the most difficult for social scientists studying the 1960s generation to understand.

> "The emerging religious phenomenon . . . was the most dramatic . . . of youth culture options."

The social and political frustrations that drove many to unorthodox faiths emerged in the context of protests against the Vietnam War—a war that became the defining event for a generation of youth and for the nation as a whole from the mid-1960s to the early 1970s. Television brought graphic images of the war into people's homes, followed quickly by images of chanting protesters at sometimes huge rallies. Even without the grim nightly TV reports, countless direct personal experiences and connections made the war's impact on American life profound and heartrending. . . .

Presidential Events Defined the Decade

Of course, understanding the 1960s as the Vietnam War era requires placing the closing boundaries for the period beyond the calendrical conclusion of the decade. [Author] Tom Shachtman, for example, proposed that the boundaries of the 1960s were the assassination of President John F. Kennedy on November 22, 1963, and the resignation of President Richard M. Nixon on August 8, 1974. . . . As news items, these events were dramatic, but as cultural influences they were even more powerful because they informed a generation about

> **Political lessons . . . taught a generation that the good die young and the scoundrels flourish, that being morally right means less than being powerful.**

power, governmental trust, and institutional abuse. As a slight variant to Shachtman's proposal, however, I am inclined to end the 1960s era with Nixon's full and absolute pardon by his successor, President Gerald Ford, on September 8, 1974. The pardon was the final event in a course of political lessons that taught a generation that the good die young and the scoundrels flourish, that being morally right means less than being powerful.

Lessons such as these—which contrast starkly with deeply held democratic ideals about fairness before the law and a belief in protest as an effective and protected political expression of discontent—have dramatic impact upon a nation's citizenry, especially their idealistic young. Although people of all ages internalize such lessons and (re)interpret them according to their individual life experiences, class, sex, and race, it is for the young that such events can define the consciousness of a generation. Members of a generation are roughly the same age, which means that their social world affects many of them in a somewhat similar manner. Cultural events, including political ones, wash over members of a generation more or less at the same time, dousing people with information that they then must interpret and personalize. In particular, the years from about eighteen to twenty-six are crucial in the development of an individual's political and cultural consciousness. By early adulthood, youth have acquired the cognitive skills necessary for politically moral thinking and have had initial contacts with many of society's institutions (such as postsecondary education, government bureaucracies, employment, law enforcement, and, especially for males, the military). . . .

Thus, the segment of the population that I am calling the 1960s generation consists of persons who were born

anywhere between about 1937 and 1956 (and especially the college-educated among that group). Technically, at least, people in this age cohort would have been between eighteen and twenty-six years of age sometime during the period between Kennedy's assassination (1963) and Nixon's pardon (1974). Moreover, on a practical level, the experiences of political culture were cumulative for this age group, meaning that youth coming into political consciousness at the end of this era had a decade of symbolism and events to internalize and to interpret. A remarkable number of political and social events occurred during this period that affected youth, and each event added to the generation's collective experience of the society in which its members lived. Near the end of this period, another new phenomenon appeared: the emergence and popular appeal of new and alternative religious groups as a vital option in youth life and culture. . . .

Transcendental meditation guru Maharishi Mahesh Yogi (center) was a popular mystical religion figure in the 1960s. Members of The Beatles, their wives, and Beach Boy Mike Love pose with the yogi in India in March 1968. (**Hulton Archive/Getty Images.**)

Religion Eases Frustration

Already a substantial body exists of scholarly description and interpretation of the widespread conversions to mystical religious groups that occurred in the early 1970s. . . . Many of these scholars understand these conversions essentially as *resolutions to a crisis of meaning*—thus adhering to the widely held but disputable interpretation that religion is necessary to society because it provides a unique sense of meaning and order to social life. . . . Rather than claiming that a crisis of meaning was what caused activists to convert to religiously ideological groups in the early 1970s, I stress a *crisis of means* within the political counterculture. That is, the combined experience of growing frustration over the perceived failure of political and countercultural protests to end the Vietnam War was the predisposing factor for the massive youth religious conversions that took place in the late 1960s and early 1970s. I propose that the conversions to the new religious groups were responses to activists' appraisal of increasing costs and diminishing returns of political action, with activists-turned-converts believing that through these religious groups they were adopting new means to the same goal.

The Protest Movement of the 1960s Was Widely Exaggerated

Jonathan Leaf, interviewed by Kathryn Jean Lopez

The leading figures of the student movements were shallow hypocrites, Jonathan Leaf argues in the following interview excerpt. Contrary to media glorification, most students of the time did not share the protest mentality, he contends. Radical feminists did more harm to women than good, civil rights radicals hijacked the campaign for equality, and rock music of the time was highly overrated and celebrated destructive values, he says. In sum, he finds, the radicals declared idealism but were in fact sexist cynics. Playwright and journalist Jonathan Leaf is the author of *The Politically Incorrect Guide to the Sixties*. Kathryn Jean Lopez is a writer, editor, and public speaker.

SOURCE. Jonathan Leaf, interviewed by Kathryn Jean Lopez, "Remember the Silent Majority," *National Review Online*, October 23, 2009. Copyright © 2009 by the National Review. All rights reserved. Reproduced by permission.

Kathryn Jean Lopez: If sixties radicals "were a small minority on college campuses and were often held in disdain by their fellow students," why have they had so much cultural influence?

Jonathan Leaf: Because through Hollywood movies, TV shows, and books, they've managed to tell a tale that reflects their own narcissistic vision of themselves as central and heroic to the time. Have you ever seen a Hollywood movie celebrating sixties counter-protesters who supported the Vietnam War? Did you know that hundreds of Berkeley students protested the "Free Speech" radicals? For that matter, how many Hollywood movies have you seen about the soldiers who fought bravely to defeat the Communists in South Vietnam? After the Second World War, Hollywood made films about the heroism of decorated veterans like Audie Murphy. Where is the film about the bravery of Medal of Honor winner Milton Lee Olive III, who, by himself, fought off several hundred NVA [North Vietnamese Army] regulars to save his platoon?

> Self-identified conservatives were a plurality on all but a few college campuses.

So who is more the representative sixties college student, numberwise?

Self-identified conservatives were a plurality on all but a few college campuses.

Your chapter on student radicals suggests it was more about sex than politics. Was it?

Absolutely. Two former Students for a Democratic Society (SDS) leaders gave me identical three-word answers when I asked them why they joined: "To get laid." . . .

What's wrong with the phrase "the anti-war movement"?

All of the most important leaders of the "anti-war" movement—Tom Hayden, Bill Ayers, Mark Rudd, Abbie Hoffman, Katherine Boudin, et al.— were very much in favor of violence and war. It's just that they wanted our Communist enemies to win. Their love for violence was possibly best indicated when Bernadine Dohrn announced at a national SDS convention that the group should adopt a new salute—of forked fingers—to honor the Manson murderers who ate and then stuck their forks into the belly of the dead but pregnant Sharon Tate.

> The most important leaders of the "anti-war" movement . . . were very much in favor of violence and war.

Why do you have to bring Barack Obama into it?

Most Americans today didn't live through the sixties. They need to know what it was to judge Obama and the future still to come out of it. This isn't just because they should know who Obama's friends—like Ayers and Dohrn—really are. Consider that during the campaign Obama said he wanted to nominate Justices like Earl Warren. As a constitutional law professor, Obama plainly knew what this meant. The American people might have voted differently had more understood that remark.

Why do you attribute "the decline and fall of the American university" to the sixties? God and Man at Yale *was published in the early fifties; it would seem the decline and fall was far along by the sixties.*

The worst of the tenured radicals took to academia as a way to avoid the draft. Student deferments continued for graduate education, and, realizing that mainstream America was indifferent to their utopianism and intolerant of their sloth, they found a refuge there—and haven't

Pro-Vietnam War marchers picket anti-war protesters in Berkeley, California, in 1965. Some argue that the media downplayed the conservative movement on college campuses in the 1960s. (AP Images.)

left. Also, grade inflation began with attempts to keep students from losing draft deferments.

You have a chapter called "The Sexual Revolution and the Start of Feminism: Where'd Mom and Pop Go?"

The radicals in the National Organization for Women supported drastic changes in divorce laws, "reforms" that did away with no-fault divorce in all but one state. And they fought for welfare policies that encouraged poor women to have children out of wedlock—and poor men to leave the home or to stop working.

What's a young man doing attacking aging (and some deceased) feminists?

I don't think most people today understand how completely different the ideologies and beliefs of Betty Friedan and Gloria Steinem are. *The Politically Incorrect Guide to the Sixties* tries to explain that—and why Steinem's ideas are so objectionable and problematic for women. She's still alive, though. . . .

What's the point of calling Malcolm X a con artist?

Many sixties movements which started out well were hijacked by radicals who gave wholly different goals to previously respectable and admirable causes. This is true with Steinem and the other radicals' hijacking of feminism. It's even more true with Malcolm X and Huey Newton and civil rights.

Most of what Malcolm X claimed about himself was a lie. His father wasn't killed by white supremacists. He wasn't a big-time gangster before his conversion to the Black Muslim sect. He was a struggling gay prostitute. He wasn't friendly with [Martin Luther] King [Jr.]. He knew for years that the idea that all whites were devils was ludicrous, but he kept preaching it anyway. And, even at the end of his life, he was a separatist—not an ecumenical lover of all people.

Should conservatives really be questioning the civil-rights movement?

We need to look at it honestly and critically. This means respecting its real accomplishments. But it also means seeing affirmative action as what it is: a betrayal of King's call to look not at the color of his children's skin but the content of their character. And we have to make clear that the Black Panthers and Stokely Carmichael weren't in favor of "civil" anything.

What do you have against rock 'n' roll?

You can respect Paul McCartney without making a wholesale endorsement of the music and the values underlying rock and the rock scene. Rock wasn't the start of music. And if we forget Bach and Beethoven or think the Rolling Stones are comparably significant, something is very, very wrong.

I take it you're not a fan of drugs or sex either?

I've tried a number of drugs. I don't think I lost my freedom or my mind, but I also don't think they were really that much fun. And I saw plenty of friends who did lose their liberty or their marbles.

I'm not against sex.

> "Rock music . . . celebrates violence, sensuality, and abandon.

What do you have against "Christian rock," calling it a "contradiction"?

Rock music—by its nature and in its basic sound—celebrates violence, sensuality, and abandon. These aren't the values of Christian people.

Do feminists hate, say, Christian conservative types, the Catholic Church, more than the Rolling Stones? Does that make any sense?

Yes, and plainly it doesn't. Just read the lyrics to a few Stones songs from, say, "Some Girls." They're pretty shockingly misogynistic. . . .

Why are you so interested in the sixties, anyway?

The contradiction between the radicals' stated idealism and their actual cynicism and sexism fascinates me.

Why would we rely on someone who was not living it to tell the history?

Sometimes an outsider has a more objective take, no? I hope, anyway.

CHAPTER 3

Personal Narratives

Angry Words from Mario Savio, Spokesman for California's Students Now Facing Trial

Mario Savio, interviewed by Jack Fincher

Five months after the Free Speech Movement began among students on the Berkeley campus of the University of California, the movement's leader, philosophy major Mario Savio, explained the fundamental issues in a nationally published interview. In the following interview excerpts, Savio says the university exploits students, processing them in machine-like fashion. The United States is run by the politics of compromise, Savio argues, and is failing to develop intellectually. He says he is quite willing to live in a society that abides by rules, but not the rules of the present-day society. Mario Savio (1942–1996) was an activist and a teacher of mathematics and philosophy at Sonoma State University in California.

Photo on previous page: A young girl stands in front of a display of T-shirts with the red fist logo—an emblem of the Students for a Democratic Society and an iconic symbol of the 1960s—during student protests in 1969. (Leonard McCombe/Getty Images.)

Jack Fincher was a writer and editor for *Life* magazine and other publications.

In what may be the largest court test in the history of American jurisprudence, 703 demonstrators arrested during last fall's sit-in at the University of California at Berkeley will be set for trial in Municipal Court this week. The defendants, most of them students, are charged with trespassing, resisting arrest and unlawful assembly.

The direct cause of the sit-in, which climaxed weeks of demonstrations, was a sudden tightening up of the rules governing recruiting and fund raising for off-campus political and civil rights causes. University officials soon realized this was an arbitrary and unwise move and modified the regulations. But by then the episode had brought into the open an enormous, smoldering frustration on the part of many who feel the very size and impersonality of their university is depriving them of a worthwhile education. These dissidents soon organized as the Free Speech Movement and found an eloquent spokesman in 22-year-old philosophy major Mario Savio, a native of New York. His own views—excerpted here from a lengthy interview with Life's correspondent in San Francisco, Jack Fincher—cut to the heart of a system he sees as "totally dehumanized, totally impersonalized, created by a society which is wholly acquisitive." Savio's rebellion is not so much political as against schools—and a society—where everything seems to be geared to "performance and award, prize and punishment—never to study for itself." Because Savio's outlook is shared by so many, its significance goes far beyond the court trial he and his contemporaries will face this week.

The Roots of the Problem

The thing's turned on its head. Those who should give orders—the faculty and students—take orders, and those who should tend to keeping the sidewalks clean, to seeing that we have enough classrooms—the administrators—give the orders. . . . As [social critic] Paul Goodman says, students are the exploited class in America, subjected to all the techniques of factory methods: tight scheduling, speedups, rules of conduct they're expected to obey with little or no say-so. At Cal you're little more than an IBM card. For efficiency's sake, education is organized along quantifiable lines. One hundred and twenty units make a bachelor's degree. . . .

> "My involvement in the Free Speech Movement is religious and moral."

The understanding, interest, and care required to have a good undergraduate school are completely alien to the spirit of the system. . . .

The university is a vast public utility which turns out future workers in today's vineyard, the military-industrial complex. They've got to be processed in the most efficient way to see to it that they have the fewest dissenting opinions, that they have just those characteristics which are wholly incompatible with being an intellectual. This is a real internal psychological contradiction. People have to suppress the very questions which reading books raises.

On Himself

I am not a political person. My involvement in the Free Speech Movement is religious and moral. . . . I don't know what made me get up and give that first speech. I only know I had to. What was it Kierkegaard said about free acts? They're the ones that, looking back, you realize you couldn't help doing.

On the Administration

[President] Clark Kerr is the ideologist for a kind of "brave new world" conception of education. He replaces the word "university" with "multiversity." The

Mario Savio, leader of the Free Speech Movement, at a victory rally at the University of California, Berkeley, in 1964. (AP Images.)

multiversity serves many publics at once, he says. But Kerr's publics . . . is the corporate establishment of California, plus a lot of national firms, the government, especially the Pentagon. It's no longer a question of a community of students and scholars, of independent, objective research, but rather of contracted research, the results of which are to be used as those who contract for it see fit. . . . Why should the business community . . . dominate the board of regents? The business of the university is teaching and learning. Only people engaged in it—the students and teachers—are competent to decide how it should be done.

On Being an American Student

America may be the most poverty-stricken country in the world. Not materially. But intellectually it is bankrupt. And morally it is poverty-stricken. But in such a way that it's not clear to you that you're poor. It's very hard to know you're poor if you're eating well.

In the Berkeley ghetto—which is, let's say, the campus and the surrounding five or six blocks—you bear certain stigmas. They're not the color of your skin, for the most part, but the fact that you're an intellectual, and perhaps a moral nonconformist. You question the mores and morals and institutions of society seriously; you take serious questions seriously. This creates a feeling of mutuality, of real community. Students are excited about political ideas. They're not yet inured to the apolitical society they're going to enter. But being interested in ideas means you have no use in American society . . . unless they are ideas which are useful to the military-industrial complex. That means there's no connection between what you're doing and the world you're about to enter.

> "The university wanted to regulate the content of our speech."

There's a lot of aimlessness in the ghetto, a lot of restlessness. Some people are 40 years old and they're still members. They're student mentalities who never grew up: they're people who were active in radical politics, let's say, in the Thirties, people who have never connected with the world, have not been able to make it in America. You can see the similarity between this and the Harlem situation.

On the Student Protests

At first we didn't understand what the issues were. But as discussion went on, they became clear. The university wanted to regulate the content of our speech. The issue of the multiversity and the issue of free speech can't be separated. There was and is a need for the students to express their resentment . . . against having to submit to the administration's arbitrary exercise of power. This is itself connected with the notion of the multiversity as a factory. Factories are run in authoritarian fashion—non-union factories, anyway—and that's the nearest parallel to the university. . . . The same arbitrary attitude was manifest when they suddenly changed the political activities rules.

As for ideology, the Free Speech Movement has always had an ideology of its own. Call it essentially anti-liberal. By that I mean it is anti a certain style of politics prevalent in the United States: politics by compromise—which succeeds if you don't state any issues. You don't state issues, so you can't be attacked from any side. You learn how to say platitudinous things without committing yourself, in the hope that somehow, that way, you won't disturb the great American consensus and somehow people will be persuaded to do things that aren't half bad. You just sort of muddle through. By contrast our ideology is issue-oriented. We thought the administration was doing bad things and we said so. Some people on the faculty repeatedly told us we couldn't say or do things too provocative or we'd turn people off—alienate the faculty. Yet, with every provocative thing we did, more faculty members came to our aid. And when the apocalypse came, over 800 of them were with us.

On the Teaching Situation

They should supply us with more teachers and give them conditions under which they could teach—so they wouldn't have to be producing nonsensical publications for journals, things that should never have been written and won't be read. We have some magnificent names, all those Nobel Prize winners. Maybe a couple of times during the undergraduate years you see them 100 feet away at the front of a lecture hall in which 500 people are sitting. If you look carefully, if you bring along your opera glasses, you can see that famous profile, that great fellow.

Well, yes, he gives you something that is uniquely his, but it's difficult to ask questions. It's got to be a dialogue, getting an education.

The primary concern of most of the teaching assistants is getting their doctorates. They're constantly involved in their own research, working their way into so narrow a corner of their own specialty that they haven't the breadth of experience or time to do an adequate job of teaching. Furthermore, what they've got to do, really, is explain what the master told you, so you can prepare to take his tests. When teaching assistants deviate from the lesson plans to bring in new material, this enriches their students; but sometimes another result is to make it more difficult for those students to do well on the exams.

On Civil Disobedience

If you accept that societies can be run by rules, as I do, then you necessarily accept as a consequence that you can't disobey the rules every time you disapprove. That would be saying that the rules are valid only when they coincide with your conscience, which is to insist that only your conscience has any validity in the matter. However, when you're considering something that constitutes an extreme abridgment of your rights, conscience is the court of

> Conscience is the court of last resort.

last resort. Then you've got to decide whether this is one of the things which, although you disagree, you can live with. Only you can decide; it's openly a personal decision. Hopefully, in a good society this kind of decision wouldn't have to be made very often, if at all. But we don't have a good society. We have a very bad society. We have a society which has many social evils, not the least of which is the fantastic presumption in a lot of people's minds that naturally decisions which are in accord with the rules must be right—an assumption which is not founded on any legitimate philosophical principle. In our society, precisely because of the great distortions and injustices which exist, I would hope that civil disobedience becomes more prevalent than it is.

Unjustified civil disobedience you must oppose. But if there's a lot of civil disobedience occurring, you better make sure it's not justified.

On the Trial

They can only try us in several ways—a mass trial, a group trial, individual trials, or some combination. None or these four ways can give US due process. Even individual trials would be held before different judges and juries. In earlier civil rights cases here, we've had different verdicts handed down for the same offense.

Some people say, "Okay, they've been crying for their political acts to be judged only by competent authorities—the courts, not the university; so now they get what they want and they aren't happy." That isn't the point. We're not complaining about being treated fairly by the courts. We're complaining precisely because we're not going to be treated fairly, because we're not going to get due process. I didn't commit myself to accept whatever the state might do to me, you know, and I'm not going to accept anything which doesn't guarantee me my constitutional rights through fair trial. 1 think it's a scandal that an action which can be argued legitimately as an exercise of constitutional rights may be punished so severely that people who have taken part in it—and others to whom it has been an example—may be thereafter dissuaded from exercising their constitutional rights.

(Thanks to FSM Bibliographer, Barbara Stack, for the work on this.)

A Girl's Experience with Feminism in the Sixties

Lillian S. Robinson

In the following viewpoint Lillian S. Robinson discusses Susan J. Douglas's book *Where the Girls Are*. Douglas addresses the media's portrayal of women and feminism as she grew up in the 1960s. Robinson also discusses the rise in strong, independent woman in the postwar era. The media's portrayal of women changed from a subservient June Cleaver type to a stronger woman. Lillian S. Robinson is a contributor to the *Nation*.

Those of us who were in the streets in the sixties, chanting "The whole world is watching," already knew that Father didn't know best. At the same time that we evoked the all-seeing global-village eye of the mass media, we were challenging—though not always consciously or consistently—the entire world view that those media served up. With our very presence we were, at least temporarily, displacing that image with something else—a protest if not an alternative. (And a protest that, as Todd Gitlin and others have documented, the media were entirely capable of framing and recasting.) Sometimes, even in those days, I wondered who really was watching and how they put our actions together with the other stories the media told them.

It turns out that Susan J. Douglas was watching. And what she saw—the conflicting images of female possibility presented by Gidget, the Shirelles, Jackie Kennedy, Patty Duke, Samantha the witch, Beatles fandom, June Cleaver and Donna Reed as well as the women a decade older than herself fighting for social change—constitutes what she means by "growing up female with the mass media." *Where the Girls Are* chronicles Douglas's sense of how pop culture's messages about gender shaped her own sense of self and how the media's response to feminism continues to influence the growing up of the next generation.

> We have learned to be masochistic and narcissistic, feisty and compliant, eager to please and eager to irritate and shock, independent and dependent, assertive and conciliatory.

Many of Douglas's observations are right on target. She is at her best in characterizing media moments that captured, represented and thereby authenticated the contradictions within the individual who was "growing up female." Hence her reading of the Shirelles and (some) other black girl groups, who acknowledged female sexuality but were uncertain how far to let it go. Or Gidget, who raised perkiness to a politics—"assertiveness masquerading as cuteness"—reflecting the uneasy imperatives of autonomy and approval. Or Mary Tyler Moore, independent yet subservient, determined yet insecure. It makes sense that it's in targeting these contradictory moments that Douglas shines, for her central thesis is that contemporary American women are an overlay of imprints, bearing, in some way or another, the fossilized remains of *Queen for a Day*, Sputnik, the Sexual Revolution, the Chiffons, Beatlemania, perkiness, the women's movement, the catfights [media reductions of the ERA debate among women], *Charlie's Angels*, and buns of steel. We have learned to be masochistic and narcissistic, feisty and compliant, eager to please and eager to irritate and shock, independent and dependent, assertive and conciliatory. We have learned to wear a hundred masks, and to live with the fact that our inner selves are fragmented, some of the pieces validated by the mass media, others eternally ignored. . . .

Media's Portrayal of Women in the Sixties

Douglas's girlhood, she tells us, was a time "when the standards for household cleanliness, not to mention for the laundry, had been raised to a psychotically obsessive level by advertisers who had read 'The Whiteness of the Whale' in *Moby Dick* one too many times." In the popular crime comics of the immediate postwar years, "the breasts of women were as large as the Enola Gay." The population of early-sixties TV included "the overly fertile and supposedly musical King family." The language of one skincare ad of the eighties sounded "as if it had been written by Alexander Haig." When the cover of *Glamour* "promised to explain 'Why 15 Million Women Own Guns,'" Douglas says, "I figure it's to shoot everyone involved in the campaign to make us think we need buns of steel." For she is a media critic and, as such, admits, "I am not a shrink (although I play one in my job)" and "watching *Charlie's Angels* was . . . my 'work.' (Hey, it's a dirty job, but somebody's got to do it).". . .

In the first—and to my mind, most convincing—portion of the book, Douglas speaks for herself and her generation of (white, middle-class) baby boomers when she discusses the media's impact on her confused, contradictory, but ultimately feminist views of sexuality, relationships, marriage, family and work in the lives of girls and women. In later chapters, as the book explores media responses to feminism (from news treatments of the early women's movement through the E.R.A. "catfight" to the packaging of the issues in entertainment programs and commercials), the critical "I" moves into the background. But she never completely retires from the scene, and is present—as both feminist and mother—in the concluding chapter. Douglas is not only reconciled to her past as a media fan, she takes responsibility for—and sometimes pride in—it, as she shows us where that fan and her peers were manipulated by representations and how an opposing (indeed, an oppositional) message nonetheless slipped through what Janice Radway has called the "ideological seams" in those representations. . . .

> Her own working mother's inability to come up to the televised maternal ideal of perpetual understanding combined with effortless housekeeping had its impact on both mother and daughter.

In the early sixties, for instance, Douglas's middle-class "we" not only saw "on the same TV that brought us fictional conflict-free towns like Mayberry and Springfield, all-too-real places like Selma and Birmingham," but "after we'd watched the perfect, secure, harmonious families on *The Donna Reed Show* . . . we watched our parents fight with each other, yell at us and hit us, and plot their divorces." Her own working mother's inability to come up to the televised maternal ideal of perpetual understanding combined with effortless housekeeping had its impact on both mother and daughter.

By contrast, to those of us who were not middle class, whatever our race or region, the idealized structure and harmony of the TV families looked like consumer goods. It was what those others, the people on the screen, had, just as each fictive family had a house with a porch, an upstairs and an up-to-date, appliance-heavy kitchen. Just as they had white skins, names without ethnic associations and a daddy who went to the office in a suit and tie. We were all being told that a level of family harmony beyond what our own families achieved was the norm. But some of us—I would argue most of us—were also being told that a certain level of consumption was the norm, and we didn't have that either. If you add to the family-based series all the TV commercials and print ads where the only subject of the mini-drama was some product, the received message makes an even clearer identification of affect and consumption.

The Role of Patriarchal Capitalism

I am not saying that Douglas's observations are wrong but rather that her subjective approach keeps them partial and superficial. This happens not only with family relationships but with representations of society as a whole. Douglas does draw some sharp contrasts between the image of the world available to her as an adolescent watching entertainment programs and the revelations, however limited, of TV news. And, as an adult, she remarks on the way the conflicts in *Dallas* and *Dynasty* "reaffirmed that patriarchal capitalism was the only game in town, the only imaginable way to organize society, and that it was impossible for women, whether they were traditional wives or ambitious vixens, to put forward an alternative."

It's precisely because Douglas sees this that I want her to tell me more and also to tell me how the mass media themselves, as an industry in patriarchal capitalism, fit into the larger social order. Instead, she remarks that hardly anyone with sense "believes that six rich, jowly white guys in pin-striped suits sit together in some skyscraper and gleefully conspire to inundate all of us with the message that scrubbing mildew off the bathroom tiles is, for women, akin to a religious epiphany." O.K., so I'm a person of sense and I don't (exactly) believe that.

But I firmly believe Ted Turner exists and that, while he and his brother moguls may not be cartoons, they are a nightmare. . . .

Douglas herself argues, early on, that if enough people think studying the media is a waste of time, then the media themselves can seem less influential than they really are. Then they get off the hook for doing what they do best: promoting a white, upper-middle-class, male view of the world that urges the rest of us to sit passively on our sofas and fantasize about consumer goods while they handle the important stuff, like the economy, the environment, or child care. If it was important enough to them to spend hundreds of thousands of dollars to bring us *Mr. Ed*, Enjoli perfume . . . and *Dallas*, then it's important enough for us to figure out why. . . .

The Image of June Cleaver as the Typical Postwar American Woman

Douglas's light touch when dealing with serious matters and her choice of a commercial publishing house combine to assure a readership among those who grew up with the mass media and are looking for a guide to our most common culture that is neither a nostalgia trip nor a put-down. It's too bad that Joanne Meyerowitz's edited collection of essays, *NOT June Cleaver*, published by a university press with a fine track record in the areas of class and gender studies, is less likely to reach the audience that grew up (and some who threw up) on the image of June Cleaver as the typical postwar American woman.

In her introduction, Meyerowitz points out that for some, this postwar story is a romance steeped in nostalgic longing for an allegedly simpler, happier, and more prosperous time. For others, it is an ironic story of declension, in which the housewife finds herself trapped in a domestic cage after spreading her wings during World War II. In either case, it flattens the history of women, reducing the multidimensional complexity of the past to a snapshot of middle-class women in suburban homes.

Meyerowitz's title and her own essay—which reassesses the role of women's magazines in espousing the postwar feminine mystique—recognize the same disjunctions and connections between media images and female experience that Douglas emphasizes. Douglas focuses on the mass media from a perspective informed by mothers like her own, accorded no cultural recognition for their discontented double workday, and daughters like herself, who vowed that, whatever happened, they were not going to turn out like their mothers. By contrast, the essays in *NOT June Cleaver* move away from issues of representation to consider women whose lives escaped being distorted or stereotyped only because the media made them totally invisible.

> Women in the postwar years not only held jobs, their labor-force participation was the object of policy studies that . . . simultaneously invoked and expanded the domestic ideal.

Postwar Feminism

So, the volume tells us, women in the postwar years not only held jobs, their labor-force participation was the object of policy studies that, as Susan Hartman's contribution reveals, simultaneously invoked and expanded the domestic ideal. Married workers included new Chinese immigrants whose garment-industry jobs, according to Xiaolan Bao, transformed family and community patterns, and nurses for whom, as Susan Rimby Leighow shows, hospitals around the country had to establish child care centers. And, as Dorothy Sue Cobble argues in "Recapturing Working-Class Feminism," they were labor unionists whose struggle "for pay equity and for mechanisms to lessen the double burden of home and work should be as central to the history of twentieth-century feminism as the battle for the enactment of the Equal Rights Amendment."

As activists in a time of open political repression, they fought against the repression itself (see Deborah Gerson's remarkable account of support for the families of [US senator Joseph] McCarthy's victims, a study based on personal history as well as research). They worked in "progressive" organizations like the Y and the A.C.L.U., in the peace movement and in Mexican-American community organizing that, as Margaret Rose documents, laid the foundations for the Chicano activism of the next generation. They lived on the edge—indeed, on more edges than anyone raised on the smooth-honed media image could imagine existed—as prostitutes, abortionists, "unwed mothers," lesbians, Beats, sexual rebels and, in the memorable instance chronicled in Ruth Feldstein's "I Want the Whole World to See," as the grieving, militant mother of lynch victim Emmett Till.

A Students for a Democratic Society Leader Looks Back

Carl Oglesby, interviewed by Bill Kauffman

Four decades after leading the Students for a Democratic Society (SDS), Carl Oglesby reflects in an interview about the rise and fall of the sixties student movement. In the following excerpt he comes across as still true to his ideals. He was sorry to see certain close friends become fatally militant—and to see personally how the government abused its powers. Oglesby reflects as well on his friendship with the bright young Hillary Rodham Clinton. He concludes that the reelection of George W. Bush as president shakes his faith in American democracy. After his SDS experience, Carl Oglesby taught at Antioch, Dartmouth, and the Massachusetts Institute of Technology, wrote many books, and recorded two albums of folk music. He died at age seventy-six in 2011. Widely published writer and editor Bill Kauffman has written nine books.

SOURCE. Carl Oglesby, interviewed by Bill Kauffman, "Writer on the Storm," *Reason Magazine*, vol. 39, iss. 11, April 2008, p. 46. Copyright © 2008 by the Reason Foundation. All rights reserved. Reproduced by permission.

Carl Oglesby was the Middle American—and emphatically libertarian—voice of this New Left. The Akron, Ohio, native and son of a rubber-factory worker was a 30-year-old playwright laboring for a defense contractor in Ann Arbor, Michigan, when a series of events thrust him into the presidency of Students for a Democratic Society (SDS), the largest and most influential bloc of the student protest movement. . . .

Oglesby parleyed and parried and partied with everyone from the existentialist philosopher Jean-Paul Sartre to the libertarian economist Murray Rothbard to a young Wellesley activist named Hillary Rodham. He had the time of his life. But by 1968, SDS had splintered into rival factions. Oglesby represented what he called "SDS's freewheeling participatory democracy" against the violent Weathermen, whose public face was the cheerleader turned bomb-cheerer Bernardine Dohrn. The Weathermen won the competition by losing: SDS was destroyed, in Oglesby's words, by "the toxic blend of road rage and comic book Marxism . . . of the Weathermen." The blast that shattered the student left was detonated on March 6, 1970, when three Weathermen died in a Greenwich Village townhouse after their homemade nail bomb accidentally went off.

The movement splintered; Oglesby burned out. He went on to record two folk albums, suffused with a kind of Beat Americana and elegiac—and nonpolitical—lyricism. Always haunted by the assassination of John F. Kennedy, he analyzed elite politics in *The Yankee and Cowboy War* (1976), in which he viewed American history from the JFK assassination to Watergate as a struggle between Eastern (Yankee) and Southwestern (Cowboy) interests. Oglesby would write two more books about the Kennedy killing.

Oglesby has recounted his experiences as the libertarian soul of SDS in a new [2008] memoir, *Ravens in the Storm* (Scribner's), which he wrote with the research assistance of his 4,000-page FBI and CIA files. A septuagenarian now living in Amherst, Massachusetts, Carl Oglesby spoke with author Bill Kauffman in January [2008].

His Activism Began with the Vietnam War

Bill Kauffman: How does a young aerospace supervisor at Bendix go from toiling for the military-industrial complex to president of SDS in the space of a year?

Carl Oglesby: Easy. The steps were simple, logical, nothing strange about what happened. I went to work for a congressional candidate [Wes Vivian, in 1964], and he wanted a position statement on Vietnam. I drew the short straw, so I started researching the war and wrote a paper for him, which said, "Wrong war. Wrong place. Don't do it." He said, "I'm not going to say anything like that: It sounds like appeasement." So I withdrew from his campaign. About that time, New York SDS fought a big battle to get a subway poster that showed a picture of a burned Vietnamese kid and asked the question, "Why are we burning, torturing, killing the people of South Vietnam? Get the facts. Write SDS." People had to fight to get the poster up because the city didn't want to do it. That created a stir, the poster did go up, a few people wrote to SDS for the "facts," and SDS didn't have anything to send out. I had come across SDS people at the University of Michigan teach-in, and my paper became the document that got sent around when people wrote to SDS responding to that poster.

> 'Why are we burning, torturing, killing the people of South Vietnam? Get the facts. Write SDS.'

You go from supplying a position paper to president. That's a meteoric rise.

Students for a Democratic Society leader Carl Oglesby gives a speech at a school in East Lansing, Michigan, in 1968. (Tom Copi/Getty Images.)

You've got to remember that SDS was a very new organization, and the fact that I had just come in the door was not unique; a lot of people were in the same position. There had been a movement to get rid of the national officers on the grounds that to have a president, a vice president, a national secretary, was inherently elitist. I spoke against that, saying that SDS was going to be a part of the world and needed to have spokespeople it could hold to account. That position won out, somebody nominated me for president, and the winner turned out to be me.

You called yourself a libertarian while active in SDS. How significant was the libertarian presence within SDS and the New Left?

There was a strong presence but not dominant or majoritarian. Remember that SDS was founded to be a democratic organization, not to be socialist. Its most basic slogan was "People Should Be Involved in Making the Decisions that Affect Their Lives." That was what SDS was about. Whatever decision gets made, it should be democratic. It was on that basis that SDS cut through the whole argument about socialism vs. capitalism. We simply said that whatever economic formation we adopted should be adopted democratically and openly.

> "Principled conservatives had as solid a reason to oppose the Vietnam War and to oppose racism as anyone within the conventional left."

In your 1967 essay "Vietnamese Crucible," you quoted libertarian sorts like Frank Chodorov and Garet Garrett and asserted that "the Old Right and the New Left are morally and politically coordinated." How did you come to that conclusion?

Just by looking at the things that those right-wing guys said. I can't say that mine was the majority view within SDS in terms of that question, but I always thought that principled conservatives had as solid a reason to oppose the Vietnam War and to oppose racism as anyone within the conventional left.

Assessing the New Left from 40 years later, was it "morally and politically coordinated" with the Old Right?

Not in any active sense. There were very few connections between SDS and right-wing organizations. I can't say that ever panned out. On the other hand, SDS was never a socialist organization. That doesn't deny the fact that most people in SDS, if they had to make a choice between socialism, liberalism, and capitalism, would have called themselves socialist.

But not you.

No. I was always suspicious of government-operated systems.

Were there particular libertarians who helped open your eyes to the Old Right/New Left congruence?

Murray Rothbard, with whom I had several very delightful conversations, was one of my favorites.

You proposed that SDS cooperate with the right-wing student group Young Americans for Freedom [YAF] on some projects. Did anything ever come of that?

I got denounced within SDS for that. In Southern California, some YAF guys did respond to the call and took part in our demonstrations against the war.

SDS finally collapsed, and out crawled the Weathermen. What was your experience with the Weathermen?

A good many of them were close friends. The ones who got killed in the Greenwich Village townhouse explosion were especially close. Diana Oughten had been a babysitter of my kids. Terry Robbins had been the one guy in the world who listened to the lyrics of my songs and helped me figure out what I was trying to say. I remember talking about existentialism with Teddy Gold, spending a whole afternoon talking about [philosophers Jean-Paul] Sartre and [Martin] Heidegger and [Simone] De Beauvoir.

I was close for a while to Bernardine Dohrn. I used to stay with her when I visited New York. Thought the world of her. Still like her, by the way. Jeff Jones was another Weatherman I was close to. I never thought they were right; I thought they were pushing the envelope in very destructive ways and were probably going to wind up hurting themselves and hurting SDS, which they now would acknowledge. Bernardine, early last year at a conference at Brown University, apologized for the role that she played. Very simply she stood up and said, "I'm sorry." She didn't have to explain what she was sorry for or why. She just said "I'm sorry" and sat down.

> 'When you pick up the saber, you hand it to your enemies.'

I had it pretty tough from the Weathermen for a while. I was seen as a despicable liberal. But I never felt impeded by the Weathermen. I was sorry that they destroyed SDS. Their view was that SDS had done what SDS could do and that now the struggle needed to be escalated. It was time to pick up the gun. And the Weather kids thought they could get somewhere by doing that.

You quote Emma Goldman to great effect in the book.

"When you pick up the saber, you hand it to your enemies."

The general view of the Weathermen today would be that they were nihilistic brats playing at violence. Is that unfair?

They weren't nihilists. They were true believers. They had a passion for ridding the world, or the United States anyway, of a peculiarly odious form of cryptofascism, or militarism at least. They always were clear that they were fighting the militarizing of the United States and American foreign policy. They weren't just into violence for violence's sake. They were doing the best they could in their limited imagining of the situation to fight the people who were making things bad for Americans and Vietnamese and others around the world.

Did the Weathermen and SDS contain many federal agents provocateur?

Many? Who knows. Some, certainly. If there were no agents among us, then as taxpayers we would be well within our rights to demand to know why not!

> I was not one of the first to see that the government played dirty.

I don't think anybody ever objected to surveillance. People assumed that surveillance would exist; you just had to live with it. People were also willing to assume that surveillance would be honest, and that the government would not create, out of whole cloth, a pattern of abuses that it could attribute to us and use against us in the courts of public opinion and of law to destroy us. That was playing dirty.

I was not one of the first to see that the government played dirty. It took me a while to come to terms with that—if I ever did. My thought was, let the informers inform. If they're honest, what they'll inform is that we were an open, democratic organization with no hookup to any foreign groups, no hook-up to the Communist Party. If you establish that, everything else is inconsequential.

But I was naive. The government had its own reasons for wanting to destroy SDS. We were messing up their plans, and they didn't like us. So they did what they thought they needed to do to tear us up. That's one of the reasons the Weathermen formed. I wouldn't be surprised if the government had something to do with the Weathermen. [US president Lyndon Johnson adviser]

McGeorge Bundy said that the best thing they had going for them was the "violent doves." It was to the government's advantage if SDS undertook violent tactics: It turned the public against us, and it opened up the gates on police action.

In Ravens in the Storm, *you recount a series of fascinating exchanges with Dohrn. "I'm not sure I know where you're coming from," says Dohrn. To which you reply, "Ann Arbor, Kent, Akron, Kalamazoo." Not to frame the question too tendentiously, but did you represent a kind of hopefulness about America, while Dohrn and the Weathermen had given up on the place?*

> [The Weathermen] decided that in America, democracy was a kind of ruse. I never agreed with them about that.

I had more faith in the country's system, its decision-making apparatus. I had more faith in democracy. The Weathermen lost faith in democracy, if they ever had it. They decided that in America, democracy was a kind of ruse. I never agreed with them about that. They were convinced that no good decision was ever going to be made by appeals to American democracy, and so they tried to step into that moral gap with a set of decisions that they'd already reached. From then on, that was that. The decision to take up weapons, to become violent—that was not a democratically reached decision. Nobody ever put that to a vote. Obviously there would be special difficulties in debating something like that in a open organization. But there was never any particular constituency that was formed or sought out on the question of political violence.

There is a tension in your book in your exchanges with Bernardine Dohrn. Were the two of you ever an item?

We were very close.

Romantically linked?

What can I say? We were very close. But those were days in which a lot of people were serially linked. It was a period of open if not blatant sexuality. I was never her only squeeze. She was never mine. My marriage had broken up, so I was kind of a loose cannon.

You've said that the SDS "had the best parties, the prettiest girls." When did the Left lose its sense of fun?

A good benchmark would be the explosion that killed Terry and Diana and Teddy. There was, as you can imagine, an enormous sense of loss and shock when they killed themselves. The Weathermen didn't give up on violence after that. They just tried to be more careful in how they used their dynamite.

A young Hillary Rodham is said to have read with avidity an essay of yours in a magazine for Methodist youth. As a result, some of the dimmer bulbs on the anti-Hillary right assert that she was "deeply influenced" by the "Marxist/Maoist theoretician Carl Oglesby." First, are you now, or have you ever been, a Marxist/Maoist theoretician?

> Democracy only works if people pay attention and share some kind of essential commitment to values of honesty, truthfulness, concern for other people

I refuse to answer on the grounds that it may incriminate me! No, that's just slinging mud.

Tell us about your relationship, as it were, with Hillary Rodham Clinton.

It was a friendship, a comradeship, within the context of the movement. She and I, for a while, were warm with each other. She and I were semi-close. I always liked her. I thought she was bright and had a lot to say. A friend of mine mentioned me to her not long ago, and according to him she got a case of the shakes. I think it was because she could imagine if any of her considerable enemies on the right wanted to do her in they would be happy to discover a relationship between her and me. Especially given this lie that I was a "Maoist." I mean, no way! I was the last thing from a Maoist! . . .

Forty years ago, yours was the hopeful voice of American renewal in SDS. Do you remain hopeful?

It's hard to imagine how the American citizenry could have put [George W.] Bush back in for a second term. That goes a long way toward deflating one's faith in democracy. Democracy only works if people pay attention and share some kind of essential commitment to values of honesty, truthfulness, concern for other people, and I just don't see that anybody can make a decision about Bush without coming to terms with his failures in these respects. I can't say I'm a pessimist; I'm just sitting back and watching it.

A Generation of Rebels

Roger Scruton

The following viewpoint discusses British historian Arthur Marwick's views of the cultural revolutions that took place in the 1960s. Marwick emphasizes the role that music played in inspiring the revolutions that occurred in the sixties and the influence it had over the rebellious youth of the era. Although all teens rebel against parents, the rebellion of the sixties was against the idea of parents, not parents themselves. Roger Scruton is a regular contributor to the *New Statesman*.

A rthur Marwick [a British historian and author] believes, with many others, that the cultural landscape radically changed during the "sixties" (which he dates from 1958 to 1974), and that we cannot understand where we are now if we ignore what we went through then. He is not, on the whole, against what happened; nor is he uncritically in favour

SOURCE. Roger Scruton, "Dispatches from a Turbulent Decade," *New Statesman*, October 16, 1998. Copyright © 1998 by the New Statesman. All rights reserved. Reproduced by permission.

of it. But he wishes to impress on the reader that the changes did not come about by chance, and were, for all their multifariousness, the outcome of a deep revision in the structure of society. He is too scrupulous a historian to attribute the changes to a single cause, economic, cultural, political or social, and he is scathing of Marxism, both as a theory of history and as a contribution to history. Nevertheless, he is a serious believer in historical forces, and sees

> The 1960s, he believes, was a time of cultural revolution, though not a revolution in the Marxist sense.

them at work in this "unique" period of transition. The 1960s, he believes, was a time of cultural revolution, though not a revolution in the Marxist sense. It was distinguished by the proliferation of sub-cultures, by the dominant role played by youth, by the fact that revolution became a form of capitalist enterprise, and by the acquiescence of those in authority in the process that took their authority away. It was a time when the culture of opposition could overnight become the culture of the establishment, and when gestures of rebellion were promptly institutionalised, to become badges of conformity. Above all, it was a time when the authority of white middle-class husbands and fathers was subverted, in order to "liberate" groups oppressed by the old forms of social hierarchy.

Marwick has composed a huge survey of these changes which is more notable for the details than for his attempts to explain them. He writes lucidly and elegantly, and is as well informed about French and Italian developments as he is about developments in Britain and America—though less well informed about Germany. He is impatient with the Marxian concept of "bourgeois" society, and with the sub-Marxist intellectual culture of France and Italy. He bravely and persuasively takes [French philospher Michel] Foucault apart, and shows the extent to which the Marxist caricature of history survives even in this supposedly innovative thinker. He rightly emphasises the role played by popular music, and especially by the Beatles and their imitators, in producing a lingua franca of youth, whose primary message is one of insubordination. He does not neglect the influence of television, affluence, the motor car and sexual liberation in reshaping not only domestic life, but the ways of entering, leaving and above all avoiding it.

Indeed, almost everything that is associated in the popular imagination with the 1960s gets a look-in: [model and actress] Twiggy and [fashion designer] Mary Quant, Vietnam, LSD and the counterculture, [the intellectual movements of] structuralism and deconstruction, housing estates and high-rise buildings, [atonal music composer Karlheinz] Stockhausen, abortion, the Red Brigades, *L'annee derniere a Marienbad* [*Last Year at Marienbad*], the Plowden report [on child-centered education], Elvis [Presley], Woodstock, [French Marxist philosopher Louis] Althusser, feminism. The book reads like an accelerated video of my formative years, with all the good bits left out: a parade of headlines from newspapers which I once read in full, but in which only the obituaries gave me much pleasure.

Rebellion

Marwick is on the side of youth, and sees the "events of May" [1968] as a rebellion against the "structures", in which violence was caused by those charged with preventing it—the police and the politicians. He is a tolerant and genial guide, whose tolerance nevertheless has a tendency to evaporate in the face of genuine assertions of authority. He does not share those old illusions about China and Vietnam

> The only members of the proletariat in the street below my attic room in May 1968 were skinny boys from the provinces, huddled together in fear and dressed in policemen's uniforms.

which made it so easy and exhilarating to stand on the toy barricades and shout defiance. But he has no deep revulsion towards such acts of ersatz heroism, and he veers away from the kind of psychological analysis that they invite. The late Louis Pauwels, in *Les Orphelins*, gave a penetrating account of 1968, and it is a pity that Marwick does not refer to this novel, which captures as no other work has done the peculiar inner disorder which found outward expression in those acts of street theatre.

The only members of the proletariat in the street below my attic room in May 1968 were skinny boys from the provinces, huddled together in fear and dressed in policemen's uniforms. Facing them were the striding, yelling party-goers of the quartier latin, wearing expensive casuals and Chairman Mao chic, who would retire from the fray to a night of fornication and expensive drugs. When I asked my *gauchiste* [leftist] friends what they hoped to achieve by their cut-price revolution, I was impressed most by the emptiness of their answers. May 1968 was fought on behalf of witty paradox: "Be realistic, demand the impossible"; "It is forbidden to forbid"; "The dream is reality"—and countless other slogans which might have been dismissed as adolescent cheek had they not so vividly recalled "the despotism of liberty" proclaimed by [French revolutionary Maximilien] Robespierre.

And if you look critically at the phenomena studied by Marwick, you will discover that there is indeed something that unites them, that they are not the diverse effect of many and conflicting sub-cultures, but the expression of a single tendency. In all of them, or almost all, we find a radical antinomianism.[1] The movers and shakers of the 1960s regarded authority as an attribute of others, and a sign of their otherness. They might possess it, but we never will: growing up is not our intention.

Every generation rebels against its parents. But rebellion gives way to reconciliation as the new generation emerges into adulthood and takes on the task of reproduction. The 1960s were peculiar in this: that rebellion was not against the parents, but against the idea of parents. It was a refusal to pass over into adulthood, a retreat from every rite of passage that would lead to an assumption of authority. The collapse of marriage and the family, the spread of adolescent crime, the loss of knowledge and culture and the gradual privatisation of social life—all these followed as a matter of course. Whether society will recover sufficiently to be able to reproduce itself is, to my mind, a real question.

But perhaps it is worth pointing out that, during those fifteen years, many other things were happening in the world of culture than those which interest Marwick. [Composers Benjamin] Britten, [Michael] Tippett and [Olivier] Messiaen were broadcasting messages of faith and hope, and we listened. Youth didn't impress us as much as the portrait of youth in *A Clockwork Orange*, and being brought up on [literary critics F.R.] Leavis and [T.S.] Eliot, we spontaneously sneered at the Beats and their apology for poetry. The important figures for us included, alongside [playwrights Samuel] Beckett and [Harold] Pinter, some serious anti-antinomians: [writers Philip] Larkin, [Saul] Bellow, Anthony Burgess, [Tom] Stoppard, [Aleksandr] Solzhenitsyn. Such cultural figures (whom Marwick does not discuss) took the human soul and its destiny more seriously than the jerks and junkies who enjoyed their fifteen minutes of fame. They deserve to be remembered, if only for telling the truth to an age of selfish fantasy. And as time goes by they will be more often and more fruitfully discussed than Mary Quant or [Beatle] Paul McCartney.

Note

1. Antinomianism is the theological theory that salvation depends on faith alone and not on the strict adherence to a set of prescribed behaviors.

CHRONOLOGY

1960   February 1: In Greensboro, North Carolina, four black students sit at a lunch counter but are refused service. Their peaceful sit-in leads to a six-month-long protest by hundreds of students and others, and finally an agreement to serve blacks as well as whites. The sit-in tactic spreads to fifty-four cities in nine states.

April 15–17: The Student Nonviolent Coordinating Committee (SNCC) is formed by black students at Shaw University in Raleigh, North Carolina. The SNCC aims for racial justice and to replace prejudice with peaceful acceptance.

May 13: In San Francisco, students and teachers protest prosecutions by the US House Un-American Activities Committee. Police respond with clubs and fire hoses, injuring and arresting dozens of demonstrators.

June 15: In Japan, a student is killed and about 270 students and 600 police officers are injured in a huge demonstration in Tokyo against a US-Japan security treaty.

September: Young Americans for Freedom is founded to challenge left-wing student radicalism and to support conservatives on campuses.

1961   March 1: US president John F. Kennedy establishes the Peace Corps.

May 4: In Washington, DC, an interracial group known as Freedom Riders boards a bus headed to the South to test the Kennedy administration's commitment to civil rights, inspiring almost one thousand subsequent Freedom Riders, some of whom meet violent opposition.

1962   June 15: The new group Students for a Democratic Society (SDS) issues the Port Huron Statement. The SDS declaration provides an intellectual foundation for a growing activism.

September 20: Student James Meredith, who is black, arrives to transfer to the all-white, state-run University of Mississippi. The governor blocks his entrance then and again five days later. In response, federal marshals arrive, and a riot kills two people and injures about 160 marshals before Meredith finally gains admittance. He graduates in 1963.

1963   May 2: In Birmingham, Alabama, a civil rights march of teens ages thirteen to eighteen ends with more than nine hundred arrests. The next day, Birmingham police chief Eugene "Bull" Connor orders a group of student protesters to be attacked with fire hoses, clubs, and police dogs.

August 28: Many students are among the 250,000 people in the March on Washington for Jobs and Freedom that culminates in the "I Have a Dream" speech by Reverend Martin Luther King Jr.

November 22: President Kennedy is assassinated in Dallas, Texas.

1964   June 22: Three young men participating in SNCC's Freedom Summer civil rights campaign are murdered in Mississippi. Forty-one years later, the last of the participants in the killing of Andrew Goodman, Michael Schwerner, and James Chaney is convicted.

July 2: The US Civil Rights Act is signed into law. The act prohibits discrimination on the basis of race, color, gender, religion, or national origin.

September 29: Hundreds of University of California, Berkeley students protest restrictions on political advocacy, setting off the Free Speech Movement and a series of student actions and university and police counteractions.

1965 March 24: The first major Vietnam War teach-in takes place at the University of Michigan, as about three thousand students and faculty members debate US involvement. Later teach-ins—unofficial lectures and discussions—are almost entirely antiwar.

April 17: About twenty thousand students and others march in an anti-war protest in Washington sponsored by SDS.

August 6: The US Voting Rights Act takes effect, outlawing racial discrimination in elections.

1966 June 16: New SNCC leader Stokely Carmichael places black power over nonviolence in his organization's priorities.

1967 Summer: A spontaneous Summer of Love, centered in San Francisco, draws attention to young people known as hippies (the precise origin of the word is uncertain). The emphasis is on music and freedom.

1968 February: At a student civil rights demonstration in Orangeburg, South Carolina, police fire into the crowd, killing three students and wounding twenty-seven.

April 23–30: More than one thousand student protesters shut down Columbia University in New York City by occupying five buildings. Police forcibly remove them.

May 3–20: In Paris, students protest police tactics, occupy buildings, erect barricades, and battle authorities. Up to 10 million French workers stage strikes in support of the students.

June 15: Tens of thousands of Japanese students begin months of demonstrations.

July 30: Authorities and university students battle in Mexico City in the first of several large-scale confrontations.

August 25–29: Police clash with students and other activists at the Democratic National Convention in Chicago.

October 2: Police fire on thousands of students in Mexico City ten days before the Olympics begin there. The number of people killed is disputed and believed to be between thirty and three hundred.

November 6: A diverse group of students begins a strike at San Francisco State University. It lasts about five months. One result is the creation of the first ethnic studies program at a US university.

1969   February: Beginning at the University of California, Berkeley, weeks of student uprisings occur across the nation, including sit-ins at administration offices at Harvard, the University of Massachusetts, Howard, Cornell, and Penn State.

August 15–17: About four hundred thousand people

attend Woodstock, a three-day rock festival on farm-
land in New York State with such highly popular
musicians as Jimi Hendrix, the Who, Janis Joplin,
the Grateful Dead, and Crosby Stills Nash & Young.
The event comes to symbolize a generation known as
Woodstock Nation.

October 15: Nationwide, about 2 million people, including 250,000 in Washington, DC, demonstrate against
the Vietnam War and to honor the dead. Similar protests occur a month later.

1970   May 4: During a protest at Kent State University in
Ohio, National Guardsmen fatally shoot four students.
The killings set off hundreds of demonstrations on
campuses across the country.

FOR FURTHER READING

Books

Alexander Bloom and Winifred Breines, eds., *Takin' It to the Streets: A Sixties Reader.* New York: Oxford University Press, 1995.

Stokely Carmichael and Charles V. Hamilton, *Black Power: The Politics of Liberation in America.* New York: Random House, 1967.

Clayborne Carson, *In Struggle: SNCC and the Black Awakening of the 1960s.* Cambridge, MA: Harvard University Press, 1981.

Eldridge Cleaver, *Soul on Ice.* San Francisco: Ramparts/ McGraw-Hill, 1968.

Mitchell Cohen and Dennis Hale, eds., *The New Student Left.* Boston: Beacon Press, 1967.

John Erlich and Susan Erlich, eds., *Student Power, Participation and Revolution.* New York: Association Press, 1970.

William H. Exum, *Paradoxes of Protest: Black Student Activism in a White University.* Philadelphia: Temple University Press, 1985.

Lewis S. Feuer, *The Conflict of Generations: The Character and Significance of Student Movements.* New York: Basic Books, 1969.

Ronald Fraser, *1968: A Student Generation in Revolt.* New York: Pantheon, 1988.

Betty Friedan, *The Feminine Mystique.* New York: Dell Publishing, 1963.

Todd Gitlin, *The Sixties: Years of Hope, Days of Rage.* New York: Bantam, 1987.

Paul Goodman, *Growing Up Absurd.* New York: Vintage Books, 1962.

David Halberstam, *The Best and the Brightest.* New York: Random House, 1972.

Kenneth J. Heinemann, *Campus Wars: The Peace Movement at American State Universities in the Vietnam Era.* New York and London: New York University Press, 1993.

Max Heirich, *The Spiral of Conflict: Berkeley, 1964.* New York and London: Columbia University Press, 1971.

Godfrey Hodgson, *America in Our Time.* New York: Doubleday, 1976.

Abbie Hoffman, *Revolution for the Hell of It.* New York: Pocket Books, 1970.

Frank Kane, ed., *Voices of Dissent.* Englewood Cliffs, NJ: Prentice-Hall, 1970.

Symour M. Lipset, *Rebellion in the University.* Boston: Little, Brown, 1971.

James Miller, *"Democracy in the Streets": From Port Huron to the Siege of Chicago.* New York: Simon and Schuster, 1987.

Report of the President's Commission on Campus Unrest. Washington, DC: US Government Printing Office, 1970.

Kirkpatrick Sale, *SDS.* New York: Random House, 1973.

Periodicals

Charles Bingham, "The First Amendment and the College Student," *Student*, September 1968.

John R. Coyne, "Crime on the Campus," *National Review*, October 8, 1968.

Matthew Dallek, "The Conservative 1960s," *Atlantic*, December 1995.

Fred Davis, "Why All of Us May Be Hippies Someday," *Transaction*, December 1967.

Stephen Donadio, "Black Power at Columbia," *Commentary*, vol. 46, no. 3, September 1968, pp. 67–76.

"Education: Down-to-Earth Idealism," *Time*, May 17, 1963.

Jonathan B. Fenderson, "Harlem vs. Columbia University: Black Student Power in the Late 1960s," *Black Scholar*, vol. 40, no. 2, Summer 2010, p. 79.

Kenneth W. Goings, "The Kent State Tragedy: Why Did It Happen? Why It Could Happen Again," *Education Digest*, vol. 56, no. 2, October 1990, p. 57.

Helen Lefkowitz Horowitz, "The 1960s and the Transformation of Campus Cultures," *History of Education Quarterly*, vol. 26, no. 1, Spring 1986, pp. 1–38.

Anthony W. James, "A Demand for Racial Equality: The 1970 Black Student Protest at the University of Mississippi," *Journal of Mississippi History*, vol. 57, no. 2, 1995, pp. 97–120.

Terence Kissack, "Freaking Fag Revolutionaries: New York's Gay Liberation Front, 1969–1971," *Radical History Review*, vol. 62, 1995, pp. 104–134.

Charles F. Longino Jr., "Draft Lottery Numbers and Student Opposition to War," *Sociology of Education*, vol. 46, no. 4, Autumn 1973, pp. 499–506.

Marshall W. Meyer, "Harvard Students in the Midst of Crisis: A Note on the Sources of Leftism," *Sociology of Education*, vol. 46, no. 2, Spring 1973, 203–218.

Steve Potts, "Teach Your Children Well: Raising the Next Generation on the Viet Nam War," *Viet Nam Generation Journal*, vol. 4, no. 3–4, November 1992.

John Sack, "In a Pig's Eye," *Esquire*, November 1968, pp. 91–94.

Doug Saunders, "'Précarité': Is It Just a New French Whine? In 1968, Students Fought for a More Exciting Future. Now They Revolt Against Tomorrow's Insecurity," *Globe & Mail* (Toronto), April 1, 2006, p. F3.

I.F. Stone, "Fabricated Evidence in the Kent State Killings," *New York Review of Books*, vol. 15, no. 10, December 3, 1970.

Gloria Steinem, "What It Would Be Like If Women Win," *Time*, August 31, 1970.

Emily Stoper, "The Student Nonviolent Coordinating Committee: Rise and Fall of a Redemptive Organization," *Journal of Black Studies*, vol. 8, no. 1, 1977, pp. 13–34.

Michael Walker, "Electric Kool-Aid Marketing Trip," *New York Times*, March 18, 2011.

Jon Wiener, "Sixtysomething: Looking Back, Moving Ahead," *Nation*, March 26, 1988, p. 421.

Websites

The Free Speech Movement Archives (www.fsm-a.org). A helpfully organized set of links is available here on many aspects of and opinions about the Free Speech Movement (FSM). The site is straightforward and wide-ranging. Photo, video and audio connections are on the site, as well as links to relevant articles, historical context, and developments that stemmed from the FSM.

Radical Prints: The Berkeley Poster Collection (www.radical prints.org). This site examines the student movement through protest posters and other artwork of the time.

Student Movements in the Sixties (www.ipl.org/div/pf/ entry/48532). This site is a special collection created and maintained by the Internet Public Library. It lists print, video, and online recommendations for further study of the 1960s.

INDEX